ESSENTIALS

Simple

But

Biblical

Pastor Robert L. Anderson
Pastor Emery Moss Jr. TH. B.,MA

Truth Seekers Read

Detroit MI USA

Essentials Simple But Biblical

Truth Seekers Read Publications
P. O. Box 23345 • Detroit, MI 48233
E-mail: truthseekersread@att.net
URL: http://www.truthseekersread.com

ISBN 13:   978-0-9987221-2-2

ISBN 10:   0-9987221-2-x

Editing by Jerome Smith

Cover, and Interior design by Robert L. Anderson

Printed in the United States of America

TABLE OF CONTENTS

ENDORSEMENTS

It was an honor reading the manuscript "Essentials Simple But Biblical." As I began to read, I almost could not put this book down. It is laid out in a user-friendly way where laity, teachers, preachers, and pastors can benefit and be spiritually enriched by the content. This book is full of biblical doctrine with the theme and topic stated and supported with Scripture. As a result, one does not have to guess but can get right down to the Bible passage and prove the accuracy of the theme or topic being presented.

I strongly recommend this book. I believe anyone who spends time reading it will be driven back to the Bible which is something very much needed in the time which we live. Here is a book that I believe will benefit one personally, in group settings, for Christian education, serious Bible class teaching as well as a resource that can be used for preachers to reference for sermons because of the many biblical passages that are listed. What a great resource.

Pastor Robert Anderson and Pastor Emery Moss have remained faithful to the vision and directive given to them by God and that is to be: STRICTLY BIBLICAL.

Thank you both for this great work. It is my pleasure to have you as co-laborers in the gospel and Kingdom of God. Keep up the good work.

Yours in Christ

Pastor Quinton W. Wingate
Power Hope & Grace Bible Church
6495 West Warren Ave.
Detroit Michigan 4810

Endorsements

It is most essential for every Christian to become grounded in the Christian faith. *Essentials Simple But Biblical* is designed to inform your faith. The material provided is *strictly Biblical*, not denominational.

Pastor Emery Moss, my former student at Cass Technical High School, has years of experience teaching basic Bible truth. Pastor Robert Anderson likewise is experienced and grounded in the faith "once delivered unto the saints" (Jude 3). We are instructed by Scripture to "grow in grace and in the knowledge of our Lord Jesus Christ" (2 Peter 3:18). This work will teach you where to begin, and how to begin, starting with a focus upon Biblical evidence and Biblical logic.

Though this work is simple, it is not simplistic. No matter whether you are new to faith in Christ, or whether you have been "in the faith" for many years, this resource will introduce you to important principles and facts about the Christian faith you may not have known before. You will gain new insights into what you thought were familiar passages in the Bible, starting with the Gospel of John, chapter One.

Essentials Simple But Biblical is unique in its emphasis upon apologetics— providing solid *reasons* why faith in our Lord Jesus Christ and the Bible as the very divinely inspired written Word of God is grounded in verifiable facts and evidence. It is unique in its extensive coverage of the mistaken views of a number of false cults. You will learn the amazing fact that all of the false cults stumble with the opening words of the Gospel of John. Here also is a thorough Biblical study of the important doctrine of the Trinity.

My advice is *get this book! Read this book! Share this book! Teach this book! If you are in ministry, Preach this book!* This book can have a significant impact upon those the Lord has placed in your circle of influence. It can and should re-focus the direction and fruitfulness of your own Christian life once you have mastered these *Essentials Simple But Biblical!*

Jerome H. Smith
www.realbiblestudy.com
Author of *The New Treasury of Scripture Knowledge, Nelson's Cross Reference Guide to the Bible,* and *The Ultimate Cross Reference Treasury* (Premium Module available for the free e-Sword Bible software program)

Endorsements

ACKNOWLEDGMENTS

I, Pastor Robert Anderson, gratefully acknowledge:

My Lord and Savior Jesus Christ for renewed strength, energy, and courage. Without Him this book would not be possible.

Sister Jo Ann Anderson, my wife, whose love and patience were often tried during my many long nights of research and writing for this book, and for her continual support with whatever I endeavor to do, especially when it comes to God and the church. *Honey I Love You!*

Pastor Emery Moss whose Biblical teachings unlocked the door for me to understand Biblically what I believe and why I should believe it! *Thanks Pastor for your collaboration on this book project, you keep me working.*

Kristy, my little dog who missed out on the many head rubbings, scratching behind her ears, and her forfeited treats.

Vivian Barnes, my late mother, whom I dedicate this book. She cried and prayed a many nights over and for me.

Family and friends (too many to mention; brothers and sisters in Christ): for your embrace and continue support, I say thank you, and I love you in Christ!

I, Pastor Emery Moss, gratefully acknowledge:

God the Father and our Lord Jesus Christ.

Sister Mary Moss, my wife of over 40 years.

Acknowledgments

INTRODUCTION

A caller called into the weekly radio broadcast, "Bibletalk with Pastor Emery Moss Jr. the host", on WLQV Faithtalk Detroit. The caller's question on the end of what he considered was a thoughtful statement was something like this:

> *Whenever I am asked by new Christian converts who want to know where they should start reading in the Bible, I advise them to start with reading the Book of Proverbs. It is simple, easy to understand and has common sense type of views. Then he asked, do you agree?[1]*

The question and the proper response intrigued me:

- What would I have said to the new convert and how might I have replied should they return with questions?
- Would I have provided the essentials with (simple) five words of Biblical understanding rather than edifying myself with ten thousand words out of reach of the new convert? (*1 Corinthians 14:19*).

The theme of Proverbs is to teach how to live and the book gives wisdom for life. Telling the new convert to read any book of the Bible is good, but the first thing a Christian convert needs to know is the doctrines of the Christian Faith. The convert needs to understand and be able to explain exactly who Jesus is [Christology: the Person and His works]. He needs to be able to explain these **Essentials Simple But Biblical ~ *what he believes and why he believes it*.** If the new convert can't do this, as great as the book of Proverbs is, it does not provide what

---

[1] https://drive.google.com/open?id=0B5La9jT-2SAHa2VPWWxQVENWclU (April 7, 2017)

the book of John has as its purpose. John states his purpose for writing his Gospel:

> **John 21:24-25** (ESV) "**This is the disciple who is bearing witness about these things, and who has written these things**, and we know that his testimony is true. [25] Now there are also many other things that Jesus did. Were every one of them to be written, I suppose that the world itself could not contain the books that would be written.**"

Although John did not state what the "*many other things*" that Jesus did were, he aligns our focus with the purpose of his Gospel:

> **John 20:30-31** (ESV) "Now Jesus did many other signs in the presence of the disciples, which are not written in this book; [31] **but these are written so that you may believe that Jesus is the Christ, the Son of God, and that by believing you may have life in his name.**"

New Christian converts need the New Testament under their belt first. Logically, start out with the Gospel of John, followed by the other gospels, the letters, then the Old Testament and last the Book of Revelation.

The cults are coming: Jehovah Witnesses, Nation of Islam, World Islam, Mormons, New Age, and more. All with another [contrary] Jesus (*2 Corinthians 11:4*) and another [contrary] gospel (*Galatians 1:6-9*). Many of these groups with a Bible in hand will knock on the new convert's door or perhaps even yours.

It is my prayer that authoring this book, *Essentials Simple But Biblical*, will simplify some of the statements, beliefs, and doctrines of the Christian faith. Keep in mind that my use of the term "***simplify***" does not mean change, modify, add to/subtract from, or redefine. It is to share learned simplifications of "what I believe" and "why I believe it" in relation to the essentials of the faith. It is to hopefully help the new Christian convert crack the nut!

Introduction

CHAPTER ONE

BIBLICAL EVIDENCE & BIBLICAL LOGIC

DEFINITION OF EVIDENCE AND LOGIC:

EV'IDENCE, v.t. To elucidate; to prove; **to make clear** to the mind; to show in such a manner that the mind can apprehend the truth, or in a manner to convince it. The testimony of two witnesses is usually sufficient to evidence the guilt of an offender. The works of creation clearly evidence the existence of an infinite first cause.[2]

1. That which elucidates and enables the mind to see truth; proof arising from our own perceptions by the senses, or from the testimony of others, or from inductions of reason. Our senses furnish evidence of the existence of matter, of solidity, of color, of heat and cold, of a difference in the qualities of bodies, of figure, &c. The declarations of a witness furnish evidence of facts to a court and jury; and reasoning, or the deductions of the mind from facts or arguments, furnish evidence of truth or falsehood.
2. Any instrument or writing which contains proof.
3. A witness; one who testifies to a fact. This sense is improper and inelegant, though common,

"**Evidence**" is also the translation of *elegchos*, "**conviction**," in the King James Version of **Hebrews 11:1**, "Now faith is .... **the evidence of things not seen**," the English Revised Version "proving," margin, "or test," better, as the American Standard Revised Version, "conviction," margin, "or test."

The Greek word denotes "putting to the test," **examining for the purpose of proof**, bringing to conviction (Dr. W.

F. Moulton). Thus if "test" or "proving" be adopted, a firm conviction of the reality of things not seen is implied as the result of putting to the proof.

"**Evident**" is the translation of `al panim ("on the face") in **Job 6:28**, the King James Version "Look upon me; **for it is evident unto you if I lie**," margin, "Hebrew before your face," the Revised Version (British and American) "to your face," margin, "And **it will be evident unto you if I lie**," which is, perhaps, to be preferred to the text; delos, "manifest," is translated "evident" (**Galatians 3:11**); katadelos, "very manifest," is in **Hebrews 7:15**, the King James Version "far more evident," the Revised Version (British and American) "more abundantly evident"; prodelos, "manifest before-hand" (**Hebrews 7:14**), "evident."

http://www.biblestudytools.com/dictionary/evidence-evident-evidently/ (12/03/2016)[3]

Logic (from the **Ancient Greek**: λογική, logikḗ[11]), originally meaning "**the word**" or "**what is spoken**" (but coming to mean "**thought**" or "reason"), is generally held to consist of the systematic study of the form of arguments. A valid argument is one where there is a specific relation of logical support between the assumptions of the argument and its conclusion. (In ordinary discourse, the conclusion of such an argument may be signified by words like therefore, hence, ergo and so on.)[4]

Logic noun
1. the science that investigates the principles governing correct or reliable inference.
2. a particular method of reasoning or argumentation:

---

[3] Orr, James, M.A., D.D. General Editor. "Entry for 'EVIDENCE; EVIDENT; EVIDENTLY'". "International Standard Bible Encyclopedia". 1915.
[4] https://en.wikipedia.org/wiki/Logic (12/03/2016)

We were unable to follow his logic.
3. the system or principles of reasoning applicable to any branch of knowledge or study.
4. reason or sound judgment, as in utterances or actions: *There wasn't much logic in her move.*
5. **convincing forcefulness; inexorable truth or persuasiveness: *the irresistible logic of the facts.*[5]**

Inferences are steps in reasoning, moving from premises to conclusions. Charles Sanders Peirce divided inference into three kinds: **deduction, induction, and abduction**.

- Deduction is inference deriving logical conclusions from premises known or assumed to be true,[6] with the laws of valid inference being studied in logic.
- Induction is inference from particular premises to a universal conclusion.
- Abduction is inference to the best explanation.

Logic is concerned with inference: does the truth of the conclusion follow from that of the premises?

PASTOR MOSS USAGE OF EVIDENCE AND LOGIC:

According to Pastor Emery Moss, "Everything for me turns on *Evidence and Logic*. It is an approach that works when studying and following the Bible, but it also helps a person through everyday life." Jerome Smith, an old English Instructor of mine at Cass Tech, brought that to my attention when I was a youth. I was saved at the age of fourteen, and as a Christian, I started reading my Bible and had many questions. There was a Deacon at my local church who was somewhat knowledgeable, but even at the age of fourteen I was asking him some profound questions. Unfortunately, the Deacon didn't know enough to assist and provide the facts I needed.

---

[5] http://www.dictionary.com/browse/logic (12/03/2016)
[6] http://www.thefreedictionary.com/inference (12/03/2016)

Voila! Mr. Smith enters my life. This man provided the facts I needed. Facts about Adam and Eve, How and why we know the Bible is the Word of God. Mr. Smith got me interested in historical studies and apologetics. I found out that there were obtainable facts. In fact, the Bible itself instructs us to look for facts.

. *"Prove all things; hold fast that which is good."* (**1Thessalonians 5:21**)

The word "**good**" in Greek is "Agathos" which also means true. In other words, God wants us to prove all things and to hold fast to those things that are proven true.

The Bible instructs us to look for the evidence:

"…….. **Only on the evidence of two witnesses or of three witnesses** shall a charge be established. (Deuteronomy 19:15 (ESV))

"…….. **on the evidence of witnesses**. But no person shall be put to death on the testimony of one witness. (Numbers 35:30 (ESV))

"……. that every charge may be established by **the evidence of two or three witnesses**." (Matthew 18:16 (ESV))

"……. Every charge must be established by **the evidence of two or three witnesses**. (2 Corinthians 13:1 (ESV))

Anything a person says, he or she must have evidence to back it up. Then the evidence must be used in a logical manner. This is a sound approach to arrive at truth. Using this approach, a person can unlock any door with evidence and logic. Also, a person can always tell when things are not right, when there is no evidence present. For example:

- When an individual makes a statement and there is no evidence for it.
- When the evidence that an individual uses is bogus in an attempt to establish a truth.

Regardless of the subject matter being discussed, it boils down to evidence and logic. Anyone that makes a **Statement of Fact,** bears the **burden of proof.**

Oftentimes, people will want to rush you to a conclusion, but you should always insist on the evidence.

"Well, I think it is this or that", they might say. *You think it is?* That's the problem ~ **you think**. The evidence allows a person to know it is.

"Well, I feel it is this or that", they might say. *You feel it is?* That's the problem ~ **you feel**. It is the evidence that allows a person to know it is.

Once we realize that by applying the **Evidence and Logic** approach, it is easy to examine anything. Politics? The same approach is used.

"I say this because I'm a Republican and this is my position"

"I say this because I'm a Democrat and this is my position"

It shouldn't matter whether the individual is a Democrat or a Republican., what is the evidence for the position?

The question always comes back to "*what is your evidence for your view?*"

The Bible is the same way. For example, a person makes the bold statement that Constantine invented Jesus. What is the evidence for your statement of fact?

A worthless statement is one that makes a statement of facts, but doesn't back it up with evidence. Too often people let the person off the hook.

You are not charged to provide evidence to counter their statement. The burden of proof is not on you because the individual made a bogus statement of fact.

Even so, we know that the evidence shows that Jesus was crucified around 33 A.D. (1st century), and Constantine stops the persecution and legalizes Christianity around 312 A.D. (4th Century). [7]

We have the *evidence*, and the *logic* demonstrates that it is impossible for Constantine to invent Jesus who walked the earth approximately 300 years before Constantine's vision of seeing a cross. Even so, we are not required to present the evidence for what flowed bogusly out of another person's mouth. The burden of proof is on the individual who made a statement of fact.

Another Example: The Koran states that Abraham and Moses were Muslim. However, the historical evidence shows the Old Testament was written during a period of 1500 B.C to 400 B.C.

- Abraham lived approximately around 1400–1300 B.C.[8]
- According to the Biblical record, Moses was born in Egypt when the Hebrews were enslaved to

---

[7] Christian History Made Easy, by Timothy Paul Jones, PHD, Rose Publishing, Torrance California 2009. pg. 32.
[8] Myers, A. C. (1987). In *The Eerdmans Bible dictionary* (p. 10). Grand Rapids, MI: Eerdmans.

Pharaoh, apparently during the early to middle centuries of the New Kingdom period (*ca.* 1550–1085 B.C.).[9]

- Jesus birth and ascension ~ approximate (4 B.C. – c. A.D. 30-33)[10]
- Muhammad the founder of World Islam was born 570 A.D.[11]
- Muhammad reports being visited by Gabriel at age 40 (610 A.D.)
- Muhammad dies in 632 A.D. at age of 61 or 62.
- The Quran is not compiled until after Muhammad's death. (Approximately 651 A.D.).

The facts show that Islam did not exist as a religion until the early 7th century.[12] The evidence demonstrates that Muhammad was born approximately 600 years after Jesus Christ and approximately 2000 years after Abraham. So logically speaking, how could Abraham, Moses, and Jesus be Muslims when **Muhammad himself was not born a Muslim**? Islam as a religion did not emerge until after several so-called visits by an Angel called Gabriel to Muhammad, who originally thought he was demon possessed.

So, we can see that some people stay in belief systems because they want to stay and not because they have the evidence to back them up. There are people that came out of Islam after they examined it evidentially.

The same can be said of Jehovah Witnesses. There are people who left this organization once they became aware of the false prophecies:

---

[9] Myers, A. C. (1987). In *The Eerdmans Bible dictionary* (p. 731). Grand Rapids, MI: Eerdmans.
[10] https://en.wikipedia.org/wiki/Jesus (12/01/2016)
[11] https://en.wikipedia.org/wiki/Muhammad (12/01/2016)
[12] https://en.wikipedia.org/wiki/Islam (12/01/2016)

- in 1914 when they said, the world was going to come to an end.[13]
- in 1918 when they said, the Churches were going to be destroyed.
- in 1925 when they said, Abraham, Isaac, and Jacob were going to rise from the dead in California.[14]
- in 1975 when they said, the world was going to come to an end.

If you make all these false prophecies of which none came to pass, the evidence demonstrates a lying organization, and logic says they can't be representing the true God. But the people who stay there disregard what the evidence says.

Pastor Moss stated, "Once I made up my mind not to be like that, for me it was the beginning of apologetics."

These are two of the most devastating things a person can ever ask: **What is your belief based on** and **why do you believe it**? If a person can't answer these two questions, they don't need to be married, working at a job, or anything. A person must have facts [evidence] and logic.

So many times, people waste their time arguing back and forth, never allowing or insisting that the other people prove their points. Remember, anyone who makes a statement of fact bears the burden of proof. And yet, they have the other person doing all the talking on a nonfactual statement made without supporting evidence. There is only one thing the person should be saying: **give me the facts and the evidence**. Simply asking for the facts and the evidence would shock you at how short such discussions will become.

[13] http://www.religioustolerance.org/witness8a.htm (April 26, 2017)
[14] http://www.watchman.org/articles/jehovahs-witnesses/comparing-jehovahs-witnesses-history-with-jehovahs-witnesses-history/ (April 26, 2017)

CHAPTER TWO

GOSPEL OF JOHN CHAPTER ONE:

THE WORD LOGOS:

Logos. English transliteration of a Greek term for "word." The term is significant because in John's writings it refers to Jesus. The prologue of John's Gospel (1:1, 14) and the beginning of 1 John (1:1) use *logos* to show how Jesus can be God and yet be an expression of God in the world. The divine Word took on human form and became a historical personage. Logos is also the title of Christ in the vision of his divine glory (Revelation 19:13). Writers outside the NT, such as Philo of Alexandria, used the term but with a different meaning.[15]

The Meaning of *Logos* in the Bible
The standard rendering of *logos* in English is "word." This holds true in English regardless of whether *logos* is used in a mundane or technical sense. Over the centuries, and in a variety of languages, other suggestions have been made—such as the recent idea of rendering *logos* as "message" in English—but none have stuck with any permanency. Because of its semantic range, *logos* has been linked to or contrasted with a wide variety of other words for "word," including:

- דָּבָר (*davar*)
- מֵימְרָא (*meimera'*)
- ῥῆμα (*rhēma*)
- σοφία (*sophia*)
- *sermo*
- *verbum*

The wide semantic range of "word" in most Western languages allows *logos* to be translated in its most basic sense, "word."

---

[15] Elwell, W. A., & Beitzel, B. J. (1988). Logos. In *Baker encyclopedia of the Bible* (Vol. 2, p. 1346). Grand Rapids, MI: Baker Book House.

There are three primary uses for the word *logos* in the New Testament:

1. *Logos* in its standard meaning designates a word, speech or the act of speaking (Acts 7:22).
2. *Logos* in its special meaning refers to the special revelation of God to people (Mark 7:13).
3. **Logos in its unique meaning personifies the revelation of God as Jesus the Messiah (John 1:14).**[16]

PROBLEMATIC USES OF THE WORD LOGOS:

There are some overly exaggerated explanations of John 1:1 that are problematic.

For instance, "**the word**" is the spoken word. According to this, Jesus becomes the "***spoken word***." Also, it would indicate that "***he was created***" and that there was a time *when* "***he was not***." If he is the spoken word, then he had to be spoken into existence. As we see with "light" in:

"And **God said**, **Let there be light**: and *there was light*." (**Genesis 1:3**)

We know that Jesus is a person. One of the persons of the Godhead, and not just a spoken word.

1) To say that he is a spoken word indicates he is not a person.
2) To say that he is a spoken word indicates there was a time when he was not.

But the Bible demonstrates this is false. John was very precise in his writing and he provided everything we needed in John chapter 1 verse 1, even though we could

---

[16] Estes, D. (2016). Logos. In J. D. Barry, D. Bomar, D. R. Brown, R. Klippenstein, D. Mangum, C. Sinclair Wolcott, ... W. Widder (Eds.), *The Lexham Bible Dictionary*. Bellingham, WA: Lexham Press.

look at other verses. In the beginning was the word, Greek meaning **Logos**.

In this verse alone, there is no need to go anywhere else:

"In the beginning was the Word,"

If we ask what the **Word** was, John explains:

"and the Word was with God, and the Word was God." **(John 1:1)**

Logically, God is a person and describes himself as a person in **Exodus 3:14** "…. I AM.." So, if **the Word** was God, then **the Word** had to be a person also because **the Word** was with him. God is a person and if the **Word** is God then the **Word** had to be a person as well. And that person was also God. The Word must share the same attributes that God has, and personality would be one of these. Verses 2 and 3 provide more light:

*"2 The same was in **the beginning with God**. 3 All things were **made by him**; and without **him** was not any thing made that was made."* **(John 1:2-3)**

Notice the text says "him." It does not say "it." The *Him* is a person. The text itself helps us to understand the context of who it is discussing. Sometimes we may have to refer to a language analysis, but not here when the text itself is clear.

We know that Logos does mean Word, but it came to mean *thought* by this time in the Greek mind, "the power of God" (the same as God). John was well aware of this and purposeful in his usage in his reference to the all-powerful Word of God. However, we know that it is more than just a word because we also understand Biblically that God is a person. John says this because it is written to Greeks to help them understand that he is talking about the power of the Creator of the universe. John places this power in a person.

THE PRE-INCARNATE CHRIST (THE WORD/PERSON):

There is no way anyone can intelligently come away from John chapter one without truthfully admitting that "The Word" is a person and the person is God based on the text alone. Perhaps this is an appropriate time to reference the term *pre-incarnate*.

In verses 1 through 14, clearly John is talking about **God**. We see John attributing things to "**The Word**" (person) that only **God** can do. Also, the name *Jesus* is not attributed to **this pre-incarnate** person until verses 15-17.

John refers to **The Word** as **He** (verse 1:2) and **Him** (verses 1:3-4). John illustrates the preexistence of Christ before taking on flesh and becoming a man:

- **The Deity of pre-incarnate Christ (*John 1: 1-2*)**
- **The pre-incarnate Work of Christ (*John 1: 3-5*)**

Comprehending the text (**Exegesis**), John introduces us to what (who) has always been. He that has no beginning, "**The Word**," was in the beginning **of creation**. We know this because John informs us that **all things were made by him** (*John 1:3*) and that **the world was made by him** (*John 1:10*).

We understand that it is Scripture that interprets, verifies, and witnesses Scripture, and to prove this point we will demonstrate that Colossians does just that:

"*In whom we have redemption **through his blood**, even the forgiveness of sins:* ¹⁵ ***Who is the image of the invisible God**, the firstborn of every creature:* ¹⁶"

For by him were all things created, that are in heaven, and that are in earth, visible and invisible, whether they be thrones, or dominions, or principalities, or powers: all things were created by him, and for him: [17] And he is before all things, and by him all things consist." **(Colossians 1:14-17)**

"In the beginning was the Word, and the Word was with God, and the Word was God. [2] *The same was in the beginning with God.* [3] *All things were made by him; and without him was not any thing made that was made."* **(John 1:1-2)**

John not only states **The Word** was in the beginning, but he declares that **The Word** was with **God (*John 1:1*)**. Surely, John is not asserting there are two supreme Gods or two creators! No! He then states that this very **Word** was **God**. John is a Jewish prophet and Scripturally aware:

- *"Thou shalt have **no other gods before me**."* **(Exodus 20:3)**
- *"Look unto me, and be ye saved, all the ends of the earth: **for I am God, and there is none else**."* **(Isaiah 45:22)**
- *"Thus saith the Lord the King of Israel, and his redeemer the Lord of hosts; **I am the first**, and **I am the last**; and **beside me there is no God**."* **(Isaiah 44:6)**

The last book of the Bible, Revelation, agrees with this assessment where John reports the very words of Jesus Himself:

- "**I am Alpha** and **Omega**, the **beginning** and the **ending**, saith the Lord..." **(Revelation 1: 8)**.
- "... **I am Alpha** and **Omega**, the **first** and the **last**: ..." **(Revelation 1:11)**
- "... **I am the first** and the **last**:" **(Revelation 1:17)**

Could this be that John is speaking about two of the three persons in the Godhead: The Father, Son, and the Holy Spirit? Notice the consistency of John 1:2 with what John reports that Jesus, the Son of God, says to God the Father in **John 17:5**:

"*And now, O* **Father***, glorify thou* **me** *with thine own self with the glory which* **I had with thee before the world was**." (**John 17:5**)

"*He was in* **the beginning** *with God*." (**John 1:2** (ESV))

There is one and only one Biblical explanation that explains this: the concept of the Trinity (more on this later).

THE INCARNATE CHRIST (THE WORD ~ FLESH):

"*And* **the Word became flesh** *and dwelt among us, and we have seen his glory, glory as of* **the only Son from the Father***, full of grace and truth*." (**John 1:14** (ESV))

- **The Incarnation of Christ (*John 1:14-18*)**
- **Incarnation.** Literally, "in flesh." Theologically, the doctrine that in Jesus of Nazareth God took on human flesh and became the divine God-man.[17]

"*For God so loved the world, that* **he gave his only begotten Son***, that whosoever believeth in him should not perish, but have everlasting life*." (**John 3:16**)

3439 *monogenés* (from 3411 /*misthōtós*, "one-and-only" and 1085 /*génos*, "offspring, stock") – properly, *one-and-only*; "one of a kind" – literally, "one (*monos*) of a class, *genos*" (**the *only* of its kind**).[18]

Only the God-Man can mediate between God and Man (1 Timothy 2:5).

---

[17] Osborne, G. R. (1988). Incarnation. In *Baker encyclopedia of the Bible* (Vol. 1, p. 1025). Grand Rapids, MI: Baker Book House.
[18] http://biblehub.com/greek/3439.htm (April 1, 2017)

*"5 For there is one God, and **one mediator between God and men**, the man Christ Jesus; 6 Who gave himself a ransom for all, to be testified in due time."*
(**1 Timothy 2:5-6**)

In the book of Revelation John reveals a title which is descriptive of the person, Jesus Christ.

"And he was clothed with a vesture dipped in blood: and **his name is called The Word of God**" (**Revelation 19:13**).

He has two natures: Jesus is **Fully God 100%** and **Fully Man 100%**.
- As Flesh which he took part of the same (**Gen 2:7**) as human being;
- The Spirit of God has made me (**Job 33:4**);
- he that giveth breath unto the people (**Isaiah 42:5**);
- "For as much then as the children are partakers of flesh and blood, **he also himself likewise took part of the same ….**" (**Hebrews 2:14**).

THE DEITY OF CHRIST:

Often people like to make the claim that neither Jesus nor the Bible ever says or implies that Jesus is God. They are looking for presupposed verbiage that would not satisfy them even if they were to find it. They are blind in the face of evidence that does exist.

There are two types of ignorance:

1) **Invincible ignorance:**
   ignorance beyond the individual's control and for which, therefore, he is not responsible before God. Those who are ignorant of some truth through absolutely no fault of their own are in a state of invincible ignorance.
2) **Vincible ignorance:**

Ignorance because of rejection of knowledge. The individual chooses not to know--chooses to be ignorant of knowable truth (hard hearted). Those who are ignorant through some fault of their own are referred to as having vincible ignorance.

Example: A man called into the Bibletalk broadcast on WLQV 1500am and made an outlandish claim. He said that nowhere in the Bible did it say that Jesus was the Son of God.

Pastor Moss asked the caller to turn to a passage in his Bible where the blind man had been healed and whom the Jews had cast out of the synagogue. Pastor Moss asked the caller to focus on the context of the verses:

> *"35 Jesus heard that they had cast him out; and when he had found him, he said unto him,* ***Dost thou believe on the Son of God****? 36 He answered and said, Who is he, Lord, that I might believe on him? 37 And Jesus said unto him,*
> - ***Thou hast both seen him****, and*
> - ***it is he that talketh with thee****.*
> *38 And he said, Lord, I believe. And he worshipped him."* (**John 9:35-38**)

It was difficult to get the caller to even acknowledge what he just read. The caller wanted to jump to another Scripture without acknowledging what Jesus asked and then replied to the blind man. But Pastor Moss would not allow the caller to do so.

Also, it should be pointed out that when the previously blind man found out who it was that was not only talking to him but that he was seeing with his own eyes, he worshiped him (**verse 38**). He had not done so prior to this revealing of Jesus Christ, as the Son of God. And Jesus did not stop him or say "Don't worship me."

Critics of Christianity are always attacking the deity of Jesus Christ. They love to say that he never claimed or said these three words, "*I Am God*." But they ignore what the Father says about Jesus.

The Father calls the Son God:

"*For unto which of the angels said he at any time*, *Thou art my Son, this day have I begotten thee? And again, I will be to him a Father, and he shall be to me a Son?*

6 And again, when he bringeth in the firstbegotten into the world, he saith, And let all the angels of God worship him. 7 And of the angels he saith, Who maketh his angels spirits, and his ministers a flame of fire. 8 But unto the Son he saith, Thy throne, O God, is for ever and ever: a sceptre of righteousness is the sceptre of thy kingdom." **(Hebrews 1:5-8)**

The Old Testament prophets prophesied that Son who would be manifested in the flesh is God:

"*For unto us a child is born, unto us a son is given: and the government shall be upon his shoulder: and **his name shall be called** Wonderful, Counsellor, **The mighty God**, **The everlasting Father**, **The Prince of Peace**.*" **(Isaiah 9:6)**

'*The Targum, a simplified paraphrase of the Old Testament Scriptures utilized by the ancient Jews, rendered Isaiah 9:6, "His name has been called from of old, Wonderful Counselor, Mighty God, he who lives forever."23 The ancient Jews considered the phrase **"Father of eternity"** as indicating the eternality of the Messiah.*'[19]

---

[19] Geisler, Norman L.; Meister, Chad V.. Reasons for Faith (Foreword by Lee Strobel): Making a Case for the Christian Faith (pp. 340-341). Crossway. Kindle Edition.

Jesus the Son of God (the Father) **claims the very eternal substance, essence, and nature of God** (the Father)**:**

*"I am Alpha and Omega, the beginning and the ending, saith the Lord, which is, and which was, and which is to come, **the Almighty**."* (**Revelation 1:8**, **17**, **18**)

"Have this mind among yourselves, which is yours in Christ Jesus, [6] who, though

- ***he was in the form of*** *(being in very nature)* ***God**, did not count equality with God a thing to be grasped, [7] but emptied himself,*
- *by taking **the form of a servan**t, being born in the likeness of men. [8]*
- *And being found in **human form**,*

he humbled himself by becoming obedient to the point of death, even death on a cross. [9] Therefore God has highly exalted him and bestowed on him the name that is above every name, [10] so that at the name of Jesus every knee should bow, in heaven and on earth and under the earth, [11] and every tongue confess that Jesus Christ is Lord, to the glory of God the Father."(**Philippians 2:5-11** (ESV); see also **Isaiah 45:23; Roman 14:11**)

The Old Testament made it crystal clear that the Biblical God will not share His glory, praise, or honor with anything or anyone.

"[8] I am the Lord: that is my name: and my glory will I not give to another, neither my praise to graven images" (**Isaiah 42:8**; see also **Isaiah 48:11**).

- *"[3] Thou shalt have no other gods before me.*

- *⁴ Thou shalt not make unto thee any graven image, or any likeness of any thing that is in heaven above, or that is in the earth beneath, or that is in the water under the earth:*
- *⁵ Thou shalt not bow down thyself to them, nor serve them: for I the Lord thy God am a jealous God, visiting the iniquity of the fathers upon the children unto the third and fourth generation of them that hate me."* (**Exodus 20:3-5**)

But the Son (2ⁿᵈ person in the Godhead) does not contradict the Old Testament, but He rather illuminates our understanding of the Godhead. Jesus Christ thus rightfully claims the very attributes that belong to the Father and therefore He is entitled to the same glory, honor, and praise.

"*That all men should honour the Son, even as they honour the Father. He that honoureth not the Son honoureth not the Father which hath sent him.*" (**John 5:23**)

"*And now, O Father, glorify thou me with thine own self with the glory which I had with thee before the world was.*" (**John 17:5**)

Skeptics are quick to point out that Jesus never uttered theses three words, "***I Am God***"; therefore, Jesus never claimed to be God. However, the Jews of ancient time were studious in the Law and recognized the very weight of these words of Jesus and what He was saying to them. There wasn't a need for them to employ the ***three words*** game that modern day critics love to wrestle (**2 Peter 3:16**). As far as the ancient Jews (of Jesus's time) were concerned, Jesus's own mouth condemned Him over and over in their mind with the same clarity of the unsaid "**exact three words**," and yet words that had the identical weight and meaning.

Jesus said:

"*30 I and my Father are one. 31* **Then the Jews took up stones again to stone him** *32 Jesus answered them, Many good works have I shewed you from my Father; for which of those works do ye stone me?*

Jews understood the weight of Jesus words:

33 The Jews answered him, saying, For a good work we stone thee not; but for blasphemy; and because that thou, being a man, makest thyself God." **(John 10:30-33;** see also **John 8:58-59; Exodus 3:14**)

Jesus said:

"**64** *Jesus saith unto him, Thou hast said: nevertheless* **I say unto you, Hereafter shall ye see the Son of man sitting on the right hand of power, and coming in the clouds of heaven.**

Jews understood the weight of Jesus's words:

65 Then the high priest rent his clothes, saying, **He hath spoken blasphemy; what further need have we of witnesses?** *behold, now ye have heard his blasphemy. 66 What think ye? They answered and said, He is guilty of death.*" **(Matthew 26:64-66)**

The Son claims the same power over death as does the Father (John 5:21):

"*For as the Father raiseth up the dead, and quickeneth them;* **even so the Son quickeneth whom he will.**" **(John 5:21)**

"*Jesus answered and said unto them,*

- *Destroy this temple, and in three days I will raise it up.* 20 Then said the Jews, Forty and six years was this temple in building, and wilt thou rear it up in three days? 21
- *But he spake of the temple of his body.*" (**John 2:19-21** see also **Romans 8:11; Acts 2:31**)

"Peace be to the brethren, and love with faith, from **God the Father** and the Lord Jesus Christ." (**Ephesians 6:23**)

John 5:18; 6:46; 8:42; Galatians 1:3; 2 Cor 1:3, 11:31

When Jesus said, "The Father is greater than I," Jesus is speaking of His subordination to God the Father, a position that has always been true, both before the Incarnation of Christ, and since His bodily resurrection from the dead and forty days later His bodily ascension to heaven to return to the Father. But subordination does not imply a difference in essence or inferiority. Jesus Christ has always been the Second Person of the Trinity, and as such, possesses the same divine nature as does God the Father, and the Third Person of the Trinity, the Holy Spirit. That is what the Bible teaches, in both the Old Testament and in the New Testament.

Gospel of John Chapter One:

CHAPTER THREE

ESSENTIALS OF THE FAITH

A Christian should know what they believe and should be able to give a sound Biblical answer as to why they believe what they do. What is the evidence for what you believe?[20]

ESSENTIAL TO JUSTIFICATION

1. **Human Depravity:**
   - We see what the Bible tells us about ourselves: *"The heart is deceitful above all things, and desperately wicked: who can know it?"* (**Jeremiah 17:9-10**)
   - We acknowledge the Scripture's assessment of ourselves: *"For all have sinned, and come short of the glory of God;"* (**Romans 3:10-23**)

2. **Mary's Virginity:**

   The Virgin Birth shows that salvation ultimately must come from the Lord. This unique birth is brought forth through God's own power, by God alone and not through mere human effort. The virgin birth made possible the uniting of full deity and full humanity in one person. This was the means God used to send his Son (John 3:16; Gal. 4:4) into the world as a man.[21]

   - "21 And she shall bring forth a son, and thou shalt call his name Jesus: for he shall save his people from their sins."
   - "23 Behold, a virgin shall be with child, and shall bring forth a son, and they shall call his name Emmanuel, which being interpreted is, God with us." (**Matthew 1:18-23**)

3. **Christ's Purity:**

---

[20] Norman L. Geisler, The Essentials of the Faith (CD) Powerpoint 2006
[21] Grudem, Wayne A.. Systematic Theology: An Introduction to Biblical Doctrine (Cómo Entender) (pp.529- 530). Zondervan. Kindle Edition.

There was no sin in Jesus. The New Testament clearly affirms that Jesus was sinless and was fully human. Jesus was without sin, and he never committed sin during his lifetime.[22]

Josh McDowell says, '*More Important, Perhaps, Than the Witness of His Friends, Is That of His Enemies*

*One of the men crucified with Jesus gives testimony to His sinlessness. In **Luke 23:41**, one of the robbers rebuked the other robber, saying, " . . . This man has done nothing wrong."*

*Pilate's own testimony of Jesus' sinlessness was, "What evil has this man done?" (**Luke 23:22**).*

*The centurion at the cross proclaimed, "Certainly this man was innocent" (**Luke 23:47**).*

*It is also evident that His enemies would try to bring forth some accusation to convict Him of wrong. However, they could not (**Mark 14:55, 56**)'*[23]

- "But with the precious blood of Christ, as of a lamb **without blemish and without spot**:" (**1 Peter 1:19**)
- "**Who did no sin**, neither was guile found in his mouth:" (**1 Peter 2:22**)
- "For he hath made him to be sin for us, **who knew no sin**; that we might be made the righteousness of God in him." (**2 Corinthians 5:21**)
- "For **Christ also hath once suffered for sins, the just for the unjust**, that he might bring us to God, being put to death in the flesh, but quickened by the Spirit:" (**1 Peter 3:18**)

---

[22] Grudem, Wayne A.. Systematic Theology: An Introduction to Biblical Doctrine (Cómo Entender) (p. 535). Zondervan. Kindle Edition.
[23] McDowell, Josh. Evidence that Demands a Verdict, eBook: Historical Evidences for the Christian Faith (p. 120). Thomas Nelson. Kindle Edition.

- "For we have not an high priest which cannot be touched with the feeling of our infirmities; **but was in all points tempted like as we are, yet without sin.**" **(Hebrews 4:15)**
- *"Then spake Jesus again unto them, saying, I* ***am the light of the world****: he that followeth me shall not walk in darkness, but shall have the light of life." ***(John 8:12)**

4. Christ's Deity:

Jesus demonstrated his **omnipotence**:
"..... ***What manner of man is this, that even winds and the sea obey him!***" **(Matthew 8:26–27)**.

Jesus demonstrated his **omniscience** in his knowing people's thoughts **(Mark 2:8)**
"Now are we sure that ***thou knowest all things****",* his disciples said of him **(John 16:30)**.
"Lord, ***thou knowest all things****;"* Peter affirms (John 21:17).
*"...... **he knew what was in man.**",* says John (John 2:25).
"... For **Jesus knew from the beginning** *who they were that believed not, and who should betray him.*" (John 6:64)

Jesus demonstrated his attribute of **omnipresence**:
"For where two or three are gathered together in my name, there ***am I in the midst of them****."* **(Matthew 18:20)**.
".... lo, I am with you alway, even unto the end of the world. Amen.", he told his disciples **(Matthew 28:20)**.

Jesus possessed divine sovereignty, a kind of authority possessed by God alone, he could forgive sins:
"When Jesus saw their faith, he said unto the sick of the palsy, Son, ***thy sins be forgiven thee****. 6 But there were certain of the scribes sitting there, and*

reasoning in their hearts, 7 Why doth this man thus speak blasphemies? who can forgive sins but God only?"(**Mark 2:5-8**).

Jesus possessed the divine attribute of **immortality**, the inability to die.

"Jesus answered and said unto them, Destroy this temple, and in three days I will raise it up. 20 Then said the Jews, Forty and six years was this temple in building, and wilt thou rear it up in three days? 21 But he spake of the temple of his body. 22 When therefore he was risen from the dead, his disciples remembered that he had said this unto them; and they believed the scripture, and the word which Jesus had said." (**John 2:19-22**).

"Therefore doth my Father love me, because I lay down my life, that I might take it again. 18 No man taketh it from me, but I lay it down of myself. I have power to lay it down, and I have power to take it again. This commandment have I received of my Father." (**John 10:17-18**)

Jesus is counted worthy to be **worshiped**:

"And again, when he bringeth in the firstbegotten into the world, he saith, And let all the angels of God worship him." (Hebrews 1:6)

"Wherefore God also hath highly exalted him, and given him a name which is above every name: 10 That at the name of Jesus every knee should bow, of things in heaven, and things in earth, and things under the earth; " (**Philippians 2:9-10**)

"Saying with a loud voice, Worthy is the Lamb that was slain to receive power, and riches, and wisdom, and strength, and honour, and glory, and blessing. 13 And every creature which is in heaven, and on the earth, and under the earth, and such as are in the sea, and all that are in them, heard I saying, Blessing, and honour, and glory, and power, be unto him that sitteth upon the throne, and unto the Lamb for ever and ever." (**Revelation 5:12-13**)

- We read in **Hebrews 1:1-8** of God the Father speaking of His Son and the Father calls the Son God: "*But unto the Son he saith, Thy throne, O God*, is for ever and ever: a sceptre of righteousness is the sceptre of thy kingdom." (**Hebrews 1:8**)
- We read in **John 20** of Thomas after his eye-opening experience calling Jesus not only "My Lord," but "My God." And Jesus didn't rebuke him for his words. "And Thomas answered and said unto him, *My Lord and my God*." (**John 20:28**)
- "And Simon Peter answered and said, Thou art the Christ, the Son of the living God." (**Matthew 16:16**)
- "*For in him dwelleth all the fulness of the Godhead bodily*." (**Colossians 2:9**)
- "Jesus said unto them, Verily, verily, I say unto you, *Before Abraham was, I am*." (**John 8:58** cf. **Exodus 3:14**)
- "In the beginning was the Word, and the Word was with God, and the Word was God." (**John 1:1**)

5. Christ's Humanity:

At the time of Apostle John's writing, there was an unorthodox teaching circulating in the church that Jesus was not a man. This heresy became known as Docetism. However, we learn from Scripture that Jesus has two natures (fully God/fully man). According to the New Testament, there are several reasons why Jesus had to be fully the God-man (100% Man and 100% God). Not just any man could be the Messiah and procure our salvation, but only a man begotten of God. We can list several of those reasons here.[24]

---

[24] Grudem, Wayne A.. Systematic Theology: An Introduction to Biblical Doctrine (Cómo Entender) (pp. 540-542). Zondervan. Kindle Edition.

a) For Representative Obedience: (**Luke 4:1-13** vs **Genesis 2:15; Genesis 3:3-7**)

b) To Be a Substitute Sacrifice: (**Hebrews 2:14, 16-17**)

c) To Be the One Mediator Between God and Men: (**1 Timothy 2:5**)

d) To Fulfill God's Original Purpose for Man to Rule Over Creation: (**Hebrews 2:7-9; Matthew 28:18; Ephesians 1:22; Revelation 3:21; Luke 19: 17, 19; 1 Corinthians 6:3**)

e) To Be Our Example and Pattern in Life: (**1 John 2:6; 1 John 3:2-3; 2 Corinthians 3:18; Romans 8:29; 1 Peter 2:21; Hebrews 12:2-3; Philippians 3:10; Acts 7:60; 1 Peter 3:17-18; 1 Peter 4:1**)

f) To Be the Pattern for Our Redeemed Bodies: (**1 Corinthians 15:23, 42-44, 49; Colossians 1:18**)

g) To Sympathize As High Priest: (**Hebrews 2:18; 4: 15-16**)

h) Jesus Will Be a Man Forever. (**John 20:25-28; Luke 24:39-42; Acts 1:11**)

- "And *the Word was made flesh*, and dwelt among us, (and we beheld his glory, the glory as of the only begotten of the Father,) full of grace and truth." (**John 1:14**)

- "*Forasmuch then as the children are partakers of flesh and blood,* he also himself *likewise took part of the same*; that through death he might destroy him that had the power of death, that is, the devil;" (**Hebrews 2:14**)

- "For there is one God, and one mediator between God and men, *the man Christ Jesus*;" (**1 Timothy 2:5**)

- "But made himself of no reputation, and took upon him the form of a servant, and was made in the likeness of men: 8 And *being found in fashion as a man*, he humbled himself, and became obedient unto death, even the death of the cross." (**Philippians 2:7-8**)

- "Hereby know ye the Spirit of God: Every spirit that confesseth that *Jesus Christ is come in the flesh* is of God:" (**1 John 4:2**)

6. God's Unity:

- "And Jesus answered him, The first of all the commandments is, Hear, O Israel; *The Lord our God is one Lord*." (**Mark 12:29**)
- "Hear, O Israel: **The Lord our God is one Lord**:" (**Deuteronomy 6:4**)
- "....we know that an idol is nothing in the world, and *that there is none other God but one*." (**1 Corinthians 8:4**)
- "*For there is one God,* and one mediator between God and men, the man Christ Jesus;" (**1 Timothy 2:5**)
- "Ye are my witnesses, saith the Lord, and my servant whom I have chosen: that ye may know and believe me, and understand that I am he:
- *before me there was no God formed, neither shall there be after me.* 11 I, even I, am the Lord; and beside me there is no saviour." (**Isaiah 43:10-11**)
- "I am the Lord thy God, which have brought thee out of the land of Egypt, out of the house of bondage. 3 *Thou shalt have no other gods before me*." (**Exodus 20:2-3**)

7. God's Tri-unity:

- "The grace of the *Lord Jesus Christ*, and the love of *God*, and the communion of *the Holy Ghost,* be with you all. Amen." (**2 Corinthians 13:14**)
- "Go ye therefore, and teach all nations, baptizing them in the name of *the Father,* and of *the Son*, and of *the Holy Ghost*:" (**Matthew 28:19**)
- "And *Jesus*, when he was baptized, went up straightway out of the water: and, lo, the heavens were opened unto him, and he saw the *Spirit of God* descending like a dove, and lighting upon him: 17 And lo *a voice from heaven*, saying,

This is my beloved Son, in whom I am well pleased." (**Matthew 3:16-17**)

8. **The Necessity of God's Grace:**
   - *"Not by works of righteousness which we have done, but according to his mercy he saved us*, by the washing of regeneration, and renewing of the Holy Ghost; 6 Which he shed on us abundantly through Jesus Christ our Saviour; 7 That **being justified by his grace**, we should be made heirs according to the hope of eternal life." (**Titus 3:5-7**)
   - *"For by grace are ye saved through faith; and that not of yourselves*: it is the gift of God: 9 Not of works, lest any man should boast." (**Ephesians 2:8-9**)
   - "So then it is not of him that willeth, nor of him that runneth, but of *God that sheweth mercy*." (**Romans 9:16**)
   - "I am the vine, ye are the branches: He that abideth in me, and I in him, the same bringeth forth much fruit*: for without me ye can do nothing*." (**John 15:5**)

9. **The Necessity of Our Faith:**
   - "For therein is the righteousness of God revealed from faith to faith: as it is written, *The just shall live by faith*." (**Romans 1:17**)
   - "But to him that worketh not, *but believeth on him that justifieth the ungodly*, his faith is counted for righteousness." (**Romans 4:5**)
   - *"But without faith it is impossible to please him: for he that cometh to God must believe that he is*, and that he is a rewarder of them that diligently seek him." (**Hebrews 11:6**)
   - "And **he believed** in the Lord; and he counted it to him for righteousness." (**Genesis 15:6**)

10. **Christ's Atoning Death:**

God's holiness and justice demand (require) the death of His Son as our sinless and perfect Priestly-Sacrificial

Atonement for our sin. But where was the unblemished perfect sacrifice? There was none! Love moved God (the Father and the Son):

Love: "**For God so loved the world**, that he gave his only begotten Son, that whosoever believeth in him should not perish, but have everlasting life." (**John 3:16**)

Obedience: "Whom God hath set forth to be a propitiation through faith in **his blood, to declare his righteousness for the remission of sins** that are past, through the forbearance of God;" (**Romans 3:25**)

"Who gave himself for us, that he might redeem us from all iniquity, and purify unto himself a peculiar people, zealous of good works." (Titus 2:14)

Sacrifice: Hebrews 10:4-12

- "Who his own self *bare our sins in his own body* on the tree, that we, being dead to sins, should live unto righteousness: by whose stripes ye were healed." (**1 Peter 2:24 (KJV)**)
- "For even the Son of man came not to be ministered unto, but to minister, and to *give his life a ransom for many.*" (**Mark 10:45**)
- "**For Christ also hath once suffered for sins**, the just for the unjust, that he might bring us to God, being put to death in the flesh, but quickened by the Spirit:" (**1 Peter 3:18**)
- "*For he hath made him to be sin for us, who knew no sin;* that we might be made the righteousness of God in him." (**2 Corinthians 5:21**)

11. **Christ's Bodily Resurrection:**
- "Who was delivered for our offences, and *was raised again* for our justification" (**Romans 4:25**)
- "For I delivered unto you first of all that which I also received, how that Christ died for our sins

according to the scriptures; 4 And that he was buried, and that **he rose again the third day** according to the scriptures: 5 And that he was seen of Cephas, then of the twelve:" (**1 Corinthians 15:3-5**)

- "Behold my hands and my feet, that it is I myself: handle me, and see; for a spirit hath not **flesh and bones**, as ye see me have." (**Luke 24:39**)
- "And **if Christ be not risen**, then is our preaching vain, and **your faith is also vain**. 15 Yea, and we are found false witnesses of God; because we have testified of God that he raised up Christ: whom he raised not up, if so be that the dead rise not. 16 For if the dead rise not, then is not Christ raised: 17 And **if Christ be not raised, your faith is vain; ye are yet in your sins.** 18 Then they also which are fallen asleep in Christ are perished. 19 If in this life only we have hope in Christ, we are of all men most miserable." (**1 Corinthians 15:14-19**)
- "That if thou shalt confess with thy mouth the Lord Jesus, and shalt believe in thine heart that **God hath raised him from the dead**, thou shalt be saved." (**Romans 10:9**)

ESSENTIALS TO SANCTIFICATION

12. Christ's Bodily Ascension:
- "Nevertheless I tell you the truth; **It is expedient for you that I go away: for if I go not away**, the Comforter will not come unto you; but if I depart, I will send him unto you." (**John 16:7**)
- "And he led them out as far as to Bethany, and he lifted up his hands, and blessed them. 51 And it came to pass, while he blessed them, **he was parted from them, and carried up into heaven**." (**Luke 24:50-51**)
- "9 And when he had spoken these things, while they beheld, **he was taken up; and a cloud received him out of their sight**. 10 And while

they looked stedfastly toward heaven as he went up, behold, two men stood by them in white apparel; 11 Which also said, Ye men of Galilee, *why stand ye gazing up into heaven*? this same Jesus, which is taken up from you into heaven, shall so come in like manner as *ye have seen him go into heaven*." (**Acts 1:9-11**)

13. Christ's Present Session:

- "Who being the brightness of his glory, and the express image of his person, and upholding all things by the word of his power, when he had by himself purged our sins, *sat down on the right hand of the Majesty on high*;" (**Hebrews 1:3**)

- "Wherefore he is able also to save them to the uttermost that come unto God by him, *seeing he ever liveth to make intercession for them*." (**Hebrews 7:25**)

- "My little children, these things write I unto you, that ye sin not. And if any man sin, *we have an advocate with the Father,* Jesus Christ the righteous:" (**1 John 2:1**)

- "For we have not an *high priest which cannot be touched with the feeling of our infirmities*; but was in all points tempted like as we are, yet without sin." (**Hebrews 4:15**)

ESSENTIALS TO GLORIFICATION

14. Christ's Bodily Return:

- "And, behold, *I come quickly*; and my reward is with me, to give every man according as his work shall be." (**Revelation 22:12**)

- "Behold, *he cometh with clouds; and every eye shall see him*, and they also which pierced him: and all kindreds of the earth shall wail because of him. Even so, Amen." (**Revelation 1:7**)

- "And then shall appear *the sign of the Son of man in heaven*: and then shall all the tribes of the earth mourn, and *they shall see the Son of*

man coming in the clouds of heaven with power and great glory." **(Matthew 24:30)**

CHAPTER FOUR

SOUND DOCTRINE

What is **Sound Doctrine**? Sound means orthodox. What we are referring to is the orthodox and/or correct doctrine of the Bible, and in this case, it is what Jesus taught. It is Biblical doctrine (teaching/instruction) that comes from God and can be verified through Scripture. Unsound doctrine contradicts the essential doctrines of the Christian faith, namely the resurrection, that the Bible is the Word of God, the Bible is infallible and inerrant, Jesus died on the cross for our sins, Jesus rose from the dead bodily, the second coming of Jesus Christ, etc. These are essential orthodox teachings of Scripture. In other words, it is impossible to be a Christian without accepting Christian orthodoxy. The apostle Paul provides a good summary of the Gospel in *1 Corinthians chapter 15.* Sound doctrine is what the Bible teaches.

It should be noted that the Bible is the only book on the planet that is actually The Word of God. No other religion, according to the Bible, is a true religion. Now they may have some truth in them, but they are not true in terms of telling you about salvation and the afterlife.

> "*Moreover, brethren, **I declare unto you the gospel** which I preached unto you, which also ye have received, and wherein ye stand; 2 **By which also ye are saved**, if ye keep in memory what I preached unto you, **unless ye have believed in vain**.*
> *3 For I delivered unto you first of all that which I also received,*
> - ***how that Christ died for our sins according to the scriptures; 4 And***
> - ***that he was buried, and that***
> - ***he rose again the third day***
> *according to the scriptures.*" (**1 Corinthians 15:1-4**)

If you don't believe that Jesus died for our sins, then you don't believe the gospel and you are not submitting to orthodox doctrine. Jesus died for our sins. An example of an unorthodox doctrine that is contrary to this is Islam.

Islam says that Jesus did not die on the cross for anybody's sin. And in fact, Jesus didn't even die, but Allah took him straight up into heaven. This flat out contradicts the sound doctrine of the Christian faith.

Qur'an 4:157-158

> 157. *That they said (in boast), "We killed Christ Jesus the son of Mary, the Messenger of God.;- **but they killed him not, nor crucified him,**[642] **but so it was made to appear to them**, and those who differ therein are full of doubts, with no (certain) knowledge, but only conjecture to follow, for of a surety they killed him not:- 158. **Nay, God raised him up [643] unto Himself**; and God is Exalted in Power, Wise;-*[25]

Biblical Orthodoxy of Scripture demands that we believe that Jesus rose from the dead.

> "*Jesus answered and said unto them, **Destroy this temple, and in three days I will raise it up**. 20 Then said the Jews, Forty and six years was this temple in building, and wilt thou rear it up in three days? 21 **But he spake of the temple of his body**.*" (**John 2:19-21**)

But some teach Biblical unorthodoxy, as do the Jehovah Witnesses, that Jesus rose as a spirit creature and that he was not in the same body: that is heresy. These teachings are a departure from the sound doctrine of the Christian Faith.

---

[25] Ali, Abdullah Yusuf. The Holy Qur'an (English Translation): with Commentary (Kindle Locations 3764-3768). QuranElibrary.blogspot.com. Kindle Edition.

If any group, such as the Word Faith Movement, is teaching that man is a god, whether it be little "g" or big "G", and he/we *"can call things that are not as though they were"*-- that is not sound doctrine. Why? because it contradicts the Scripture. A closer examination of the Scriptural text reveals that it is God (and God alone) who performs this feat:

> *"17 (As it is written, I have made thee a father of many nations,) before him whom he believed, **even God, who quickeneth the dead, and calleth those things which be not as though they were.**"* (**Romans 4:17**)

In fact, we see in Genesis perhaps the biggest sin a person commits "wanting to be god." This is what got man into the trouble that he is in now, along with disobedience. We see the serpent being used by Satan:

> *"And the serpent said unto the woman, **Ye shall not surely die**: 5 For God doth know that in the day ye eat thereof, then your eyes shall be opened, **and ye shall be as gods**, knowing good and evil."* (**Genesis 3:4-5**)

Sound doctrine does not depart from the faith. You can be at any church you want or accept any religion that you want, but the Bible is not going to change and all will be judged based on what the Bible says. It does not matter how big or fancy your church, pastor, or anything else may be. There is one gigantic mountain that no one will be able to get around:

> *"Jesus saith unto him, I am the way, the truth, and the life: **no man cometh unto the Father, but by me.**"* (**John 14:6**)

That is sound doctrine! While it may not be politically correct, it sure is Biblically correct. People are going to be shocked when they stand before God and find out that God does not care about their political correctness or their diversity programs. If God says homosexuality is a sin--it is a sin! God is not going to check with President Obama, the supreme court, or the LGBTQ, or Christians for gays. The church (some) may change its position following the doctrines of man instead of orthodoxy (what the Bible says), but God will never change His truth because God is true (**John 3:33**), and His Son not only was sent with the truth, but He is the truth sent by the Father (**John 14:6**).

The purpose of sound doctrine is to keep a person from error, and/or to deliver a person from error. According to Scripture, the only way a person can be saved is to know the truth. Jesus said,

> "And **ye shall know the truth, and the truth shall make you free**." (**John 8:32**)

> "**If the Son therefore shall make you free, ye shall be free indeed**." (**John 8:36**)

Anything other than the truth puts a person in serious jeopardy. Only the sound doctrine of Jesus Christ can save a person. In fact, false doctrine can only condemn. In the Bible, this is clear. Even so, people often don't understand the seriousness of false doctrine. Look at the language Apostle Paul uses,

> "**I marvel that ye are so soon removed from him that called you into the grace of Christ unto another gospel**: [7] Which is not another; **but there be some that trouble you**, and **would pervert the gospel of Christ**. [8] But though we, or an angel from heaven, **preach any other gospel unto you than that which we have preached unto you, let him be accursed**. [9] As we said before, so say I now again, If any man **preach any other gospel unto you than that ye have received, let him be accursed**." (**Galatians 1:6-9**)

The same test that can be used for a prophet can be used to test doctrine to see whether it be of God. Scripture verifies Scripture, and we test the soundness of doctrine by Scripture. It must be based on the Word of God.

But keep in mind that today there is so much false doctrine in the church, that people get incensed (angry) when you point out false doctrine in the church. They get incensed when the errors of their popular bishops are exposed and they take it personally. They are more attached to their church leaders than they are to the sound doctrine of Scripture. The very truth that should set people free, that truth is often viewed as an attack.

We must expose that which comes against the truth. If anyone teaches that there is more than one way to get to God, or teaches that their so-called leader is the Messiah, Jude calls us to action:

> "Beloved, when I gave all diligence to write unto you of the common salvation, **it was needful for me to write unto you,** and **exhort you that ye should earnestly contend for the faith which was once delivered unto the saints.** 4 For there are certain men crept in unawares, who were before of old ordained to this condemnation, ungodly men, turning the grace of our God into lasciviousness, and **denying the only Lord God, and our Lord Jesus Christ.**" **(Jude 3-4)**

> "Jesus saith unto him, I am the way, the truth, and the life: **no man cometh unto the Father, but by me.**" **(John 14:6)**

> "Neither is there salvation in any other: **for there is none other name under heaven given among men, whereby we must be saved.**" **(Acts 4:12)**

Sound Doctrine of Scripture demands that we warn, expose, and name names when necessary to do so. We cannot stand by idle while Louis Farrakhan claims he is the Messiah and/or Christ and he teaches that Jesus is a dead prophet according to the teachings of Elijah Mohammad. He says Jesus was just a prophet, but not the Messiah; and he points to Wallace D. Fard aka Wallace Fard Muhammad **as the Messiah all while referring Scripture out of context.** [26] Farrakhan also says that he, Farrakhan is Christ. He says the historical Jesus was just a type.[27] Even so, some Christian churches who have lost their Biblical mind (assuming they ever had one) have allowed Farrakhan into their pulpits.

Farrakhan further challenged Christians from a naive church's pulpit. He said, (with his cynical smile on his face) [28]

"that the Jesus that I know came into this world to save us from our sins. Oh, Thank you, Jesus. You say, well wait a minute Farrakhan, I thought you were a Muslim?

I am, and Jesus was too! *You never read in the Bible where Jesus said I'm a Christian! He didn't say it in Matthew, Mark, Luke or John. So, what are you fighting over saying, I don't want to go hear Farrakhan because he isn't no Christian and he don't love Jesus?*

Stop lying, I can prove to you that you don't love him. I'm going to throw a little proof out there to you. Show me where Jesus said I'm a Baptist, and if you are not a Baptist you are not going to heaven. Well if it is not there in the Bible, what the @#$@#$ is it doing in your mouth?"

[26] https://www.youtube.com/watch?v=DrHasLq33O8 (April 26, 2017)
[27] https://www.youtube.com/watch?v=3Xx9E_G6-EM (May 17, 2017)
[28] https://www.youtube.com/watch?v=Z-P-B8Pj9To (May 17, 2017)

Remember, Farrakhan is speaking to Christians from the church's pulpit! He continues,

> "*Jesus never said he was a Baptist or Methodist, **show it to me?** He said I am the way, the truth, and the life. He never said he was an Episcopalian or a Catholic, but he was universal. So why do you fight over names that Jesus never used? I am just asking a question and **you can't even give me an intelligent answer?***
>
> *I am sure folks are going to ask what has happened to the pastor, he done let that Muslim up in his church, and he says hell sometimes.*"

Farrakhan says, "we are sick people." He continues,

> "*Jesus said not my will, but thy will be done. Listen to his words. Whatsoever the Father bids me to say that I say, and whatsoever the Father bids me to do that I do. That is the perfect description of what Islam is. It means entire submission to do the will of God.*"

The congregation went wild applauding as if he had unveiled some new revelation. But no one questioned or addressed Mr. Farrakhan. On Facebook, people expressed their anger in comments. But no one addressed Mr. Farrakhan's statements Biblically, or otherwise. It is my humble opinion that we as Christians should be able to do so. You don't have to be a pastor to give an answer (**1 Peter 3:15**) and to defend the faith (**Jude 3-4**). Christians should know how to expound sound doctrine.

Why on earth would Jesus ever say he's a Christian? That would be like Farrakhan saying he (Farrakhan) is a follower of Farrakhan. Or like Jesus saying He was a follower of Himself.

- The term came into being because the disciples **were followers of Christ (Jesus)**. Sometimes before and after they were called followers of "*the way*" (often in a derogatory manner). **Acts 9:2; Acts 16:17; Acts 19:9, 23; Acts 22:4; Acts 24:14, 22.** See **Acts 11:26; Acts 26:28; 1 Peter 4:16**.
- Farrakhan says Jesus was not called a Christian in Matthew, Mark, Luke, or John.
  - The informed Christian, who reads his Bible, should inform Mr. Farrakhan, Jesus was not called a **Muslim** in those Gospels either.
  - The Christian should also inform Mr. Farrakhan, he can't find in the Quran where Jesus ever says the word's "**I'm a Muslim**."
- The same Bible where Mr. Farrakhan supposedly read the gospels (Matthew, Mark, Luke, John):
  - Says Jesus not only died for our sins but rose from the dead. Notice he didn't quote or reference those verses!
  - But in the Quran, it says Jesus was NOT crucified on the cross and he didn't die. Surah 4:157. *That they said (in boast), "We killed Christ Jesus the son of Mary, the Messenger of God;-* **but they killed him not, nor crucified him,** *[642] but so it was made to appear to them, and those who differ therein are full of doubts, with no (certain) knowledge, but only conjecture to follow, for of a surety they killed him not:-*[29]
  - But in the book "**Message To The Black Man In America**," authored By Farrakhan's great teacher, whom he never fails to mention:

---

[29] Ali, Abdullah Yusuf. The Holy Qur'an (English Translation): with Commentary (Kindle Locations 3764-3767). QuranElibrary.blogspot.com. Kindle Edition.

> *"Another error was made: Jesus is supposed to have given His life for the sins of the people, and after three days He took it back. Well, this just does not make sense!"*[30]

- o **"Message To The Black Man In America"**: *"God is in person, and **stop looking for a dead Jesus** for help, but pray to Him whom Jesus prophesied would come after Him. He who is alive and **not a spook**.*[31]
  - *"You must forget about **ever seeing the return of Jesus**, Who was here 2,000 years ago.*
  - *You are really foolish to be **looking to see the return of the Prophet Jesus**. It is the same as looking for the return of Abraham, Moses, and Muhammad.*
  - *The devils have tried to deceive the people all over the earth with Christianity; that is, God the Father, Jesus the Son, the Holy Ghost—three Gods into One God—the resurrection of the Son and His return to judge the world; or that the Son is in some place above the earth, sitting on the right-hand side of the Father, waiting until the Father makes His enemies His footstool."*[32]
- Farrakhan is NOT a Muslim of World Islam according to the Quran, for its teachings are contrary to the Nation of Islam (NOI).

---

[30] Muhammad, Elijah. Message To The Blackman In America (Kindle Locations 2045-2046). Secretarius MEMPS Publications. Kindle Edition.
[31] Muhammad, Elijah. Message To The Blackman In America (Kindle Locations 529-530). Secretarius MEMPS Publications. Kindle Edition.
[32] Muhammad, Elijah. Message To The Blackman In America (Kindle Locations 650-651; 653-654; 670-672). Secretarius MEMPS Publications. Kindle Edition.

- Farrakhan talked about Baptists, Methodists, etc.; But in Islam, you have Shias, Sunni, Sufis, etc.
- Why would Mr. Farrakhan use any book that he (NOI) claims is poison (Bible) and corrupt (Quran) to prove he knows Jesus?
  - **"Message To The Black Man In America"**: *"**The enemy has tampered with the truth in both books**: for he has been permitted to handle both books. Neither the Holy Quran nor the Bible was revealed with the intention of converting the white race into truth and righteousness;"*[33]
  - **"Message To The Black Man In America"**: *"**The Bible is now being called the Poison Book by God Himself**, and who can deny that it is not poison? It has poisoned the very hearts and minds of the so-called Negroes so much that they can't agree with each other. From the first day that the white race received the Divine Scripture, they started tampering with its truth to make it suit themselves, and blind the black man."*[34]
- Louis Farrakhan is a liar and the truth is not in him. Hopefully, the Bible verses and extra-biblical information above will help others to explain Mr. Farrakhan's dilemma with us Christians.[35]

Many churches have allowed the wolf into the hen house. There will be a day of reckoning. Contrary to popular belief, false doctrine can send people to hell.

---

[33] Muhammad, Elijah. Message To The Blackman In America (Kindle Locations 2012-2014). Secretarius MEMPS Publications. Kindle Edition.
[34] Muhammad, Elijah. Message To The Blackman In America (Kindle Locations 2097-2099). Secretarius MEMPS Publications. Kindle Edition.
[35] https://www.youtube.com/watch?v=Z-P-B8Pj9To (May 16, 2017)

Oh, that's just Farrakhan some will say. He will never be allowed to come to my church.

But what about Dr. Cindy Trimm and her book "**Commanding Your Morning**?" Really, can you command your morning?

> *"Hast thou commanded the morning since thy days; and caused the dayspring to know his place;"* (**Job 38:12**)

Is God saying to Job, "**why aren't you commanding your morning, Job**" or is God showing His Sovereignty for Job to consider? Notice the context of all the questions God asked of Job (**Job 38; 39**).

In fact, the very context of Scripture demonstrates that not only Job, but you can't command your morning either:

"1 Then the Lord answered Job out of the whirlwind, and said, 2

- ***Who is this*** *that darkeneth counsel **by words without knowledge**? 3*
- *Gird up now thy loins **like a man**;*
- *for **I will demand of thee**, and **answer thou me**. 4*
- ***Where wast thou*** *when I laid the foundations of the earth?*
- *declare, **if thou hast understanding**."* (Job 38:1-4)

"You are in charge of taking control of your day from its very beginning--something I call "commanding your morning"--and as you do, know that whatever begins with God has to end right. My prayer for you is that as you read the following pages, God will reveal the power within you--and that your hope of glory would be made more real as you learn to command your morning through the wisdom of His truth every single day.

No matter how good or bad your life is, every circumstance can change for the best if you learn how to command your morning before your day begins."[36]

And what about **Iyanla Vanzant,** the Yoruban Priestess, ordained New Thought minister, talk show host, doctoral candidate, spiritual life counselor and author of several best-selling books mostly geared toward the African American community?

In her book, **"The Spirit of a Man,"** she says she lives by an ancient African belief system where the **Father is the sun** and the **Mother is the moon**. She says she studied "A Course in Miracles which is a psychological paradigm for facilitating a shift in perceptions." [37]

- She believes it is ok to worship your ancestors.[38]
- She relates to Eastern Tradition of Karma. [39]
- She believes in calling on the dead. [40]
- She believes it does not matter which sacred text you use in your rituals, whether the Bible or the Koran.[41]
- She quotes Louis Farrakhan[42]
- She believes the Spirit in humans is the "I AM" consciousness.[43]
- She believes in the Self within for spiritual salvation.[44]
- She sums up the breath of God as the same as Allah.[45]

[36] Cindy Trimm. Commanding Your Morning: Unleash the Power of God in Your Life (Kindle Locations 88-91). Kindle Edition.
[37] Iyanla Vanzant, The Spirit of a MAN: A Vision of Transformation for Black Men and the Women Who Love Them,(HarperCollins Publishers Inc: 1996), xxii.
[38] Ibid., 78
[39] Ibid., 78
[40] Ibid., 79
[41] Ibid., 80, 246
[42] Ibid., 87
[43] Ibid., 93
[44] Ibid., 107
[45] Ibid., 115

- She says you cannot get to the Father without coming through the Mother. God is both Masculine and feminine energy.[46]
- She believes in Christ Consciousness.[47]
- She believes in praying to yourself (the divine self).[48]
- She believes that the self is the part of God that you are; and the self is the I that you are when you say "I Am."[49]
- She believes in the Law of Attraction.[50]
- She believes the Moon is God, The Sun is God, and the Wind is God.[51]
- Last in her glossary: Atonement is defined to become one. Alignment with the divine within self.[52]

Even so, many so-called born again Christian women flock to the arenas and auditoriums to hear Dr. Trimm or Dr. Vanzant when either come to town. Many live by these women's books as principles for life and success, even though their teachings contradict and are in violation of Scripture. Water and oil do not mix! Churches and Praise radio stations, with no discernment, promote these books and seminars of Satan.

The orthodox teachings of the Bible take away the guess work and imaginary truth. Discerning and understanding sound doctrine causes the warning flag to be raised when others present another Jesus (**2 Corinthians 11:4**) and/or another gospel [not that there is another] (**Galatians 1:6-7**).

Sound doctrine makes it unmistakable and irrefutable that people do worship false gods, which are in fact not God.

---

[46] Ibid., 136
[47] Ibid., 140, 270
[48] Ibid., 154
[49] Ibid., 185
[50] Ibid., 214
[51] Ibid., 234
[52] Ibid., 234

Hence, we do not all worship the same God. If it is not the God of Biblical Orthodoxy, it is a worship of nothing. But Jesus said,

> "*Ye worship ye know not what:* **we know what we worship: for salvation is of the Jews.** *23 But the hour cometh, and now is,* **when the true worshippers shall worship the Father in spirit and in truth***: for the Father seeketh such to worship him.* *24* **God is a Spirit: and they that worship him must worship him in spirit and in truth**." (John 4:22-24)

Simply stated, sound doctrine is:

1. Teaching that can be tested by the Word of God
2. Teaching that can be distinguished from the commandments of men.
3. Teaching whose source is not from the will (mind) of man.
4. Teaching authorized by **God the Father (John 7:15, 16)**.
   a. Teaching that the **Son of God** delivered unmodified, uncorrupted and with authority (**John 16:15**).
      i. Teaching that the **Holy Spirit** delivered unmodified, uncorrupted and with authority (**John 14:26; 15:26-27; 16:13-14**).
      ii. One God; three persons (Father, Son, Holy Spirit); One doctrine; One truth.
   b. The truth of God that can be Biblically verified.
5. Last, but not least, Sound Doctrine, if it is sound:
   a. always points to and leads to Jesus Christ. And not a **Christ want to be**, or **counterfeit**. (**2 Corinthians 11:3-4**)
   b. Does not distort the Gospel of Jesus Christ (**Galatians 1:6-12**).
   c. Does not demote Christ to elevate man.

(2 Corinthians 11:12-15)

The Godhead [tri-unity (persons)] is always in agreement. We see clearly in Scripture, that what the Father says, the Son says likewise; What the Son says, the Holy Spirit likewise says. Sound Doctrine has the harmony of Scripture and the Tri-unity of God. Jesus, the God-man, is fully God and fully man,

An examination of Scripture verifies it is Scripture that witnesses Jesus did not bring a new doctrine. He says, the Scripture testified of me (**John 5:39**). The Scripture is sent by the will of God (**2 Peter 1:21**) and the Son came by the will of God (**John 3:16**). Jesus taught and authorized His disciples and Apostles and He sent them with Sound Doctrine.

Time does not change the truth of God, His principles, His commandments, or His doctrine. The Father puts His doctrine into the hands of His only begotten Son (**John 7:16**).

On earth, Jesus is responding and doing everything that the Father has told him to do. In other words:

- If you stand against me (the Son ~2nd person of the Godhead), you are standing against God (the Father ~ 1st person of the Godhead).
- If you reject me (the Son ~2nd person of the Godhead), you are rejecting God (the Father ~ 1st person of the Godhead).
- In the Incarnation the Son is subordinating himself.

JESUS CHRIST HAD AND TAUGHT DOCTRINE:
- "And they were astonished at his Doctrine: for **he taught them as one that had authority**, and not as the scribes." (**Mark 1:22**)
- "And he taught them many things by parables, and said unto them in his Doctrine," (**Mark 4:2**)

- "And **he said unto them in his Doctrine**, Beware of the scribes, which love to go in long clothing, and love salutations in the marketplaces," (**Mark 12:38**)

THE DOCTRINE OF GOD, JESUS, CHRIST: ONE DOCTRINE:

- "*Jesus answered them, and said, My Doctrine is not mine, but his that sent me.*" (**John 7:16**)
- "*If any man will do his will, he shall know of the Doctrine, whether it be of God, or whether I speak of myself.*" (**John 7:17**)
- "*Not purloining, but shewing all good fidelity; that they may adorn the Doctrine of God our Saviour in all things.*" (**Titus 2:10**)
- "*All scripture is given by inspiration of God, and **is profitable for** Doctrine, for reproof, for correction, for instruction in righteousness:*" (**2 Timothy 3:16**)
- "*My Doctrine shall drop as the rain, my speech shall distil as the dew, as the small rain upon the tender herb, and as the showers upon the grass:*" (**Deuteronomy 32:2**)

THE TROUBLE OF NOT ABIDING IN SOUND DOCTRINE:

- "*Therefore leaving the principles of the Doctrine of Christ, let us go on unto perfection; not laying again the foundation of repentance from dead works, and of faith toward God,*" (**Hebrews 6:1**)
- "*Whosoever transgresseth, and abideth not in the Doctrine of Christ, hath not God. He that abideth in the Doctrine of Christ, **he hath both the Father and the Son.**" (**2 John 1:9**)

THE APOSTLES TAUGHT SOUND DOCTRINE:

The Apostles received their doctrine from Jesus Christ. The title "Apostle's Doctrine" does not mean that they had their own doctrine or another doctrine. For example: "***The Revelation of Jesus Christ,** which God gave unto him, **to shew unto his servants** things which must shortly come to pass; **and he sent and signified it by his angel unto his servant John**: 2 Who bare record of* *the word of God, and of the testimony of Jesus Christ, and of all things that he saw."* (**Revelation 1:1-2**)

"And I said, What shall I do, Lord? And the Lord said unto me, **Arise, and go into Damascus; and there it shall be told thee of all things which are appointed for thee to do**. (**Acts 22:10**)

"I have shewed you all things, how that so labouring ye ought to support the weak, and to remember the words of the Lord Jesus, how he said, **It is more blessed to give than to receive**." (**Acts 20:35**)

"And it came to pass, that, when I was come again to Jerusalem, even while I prayed in the temple, I was in a trance; [18] *And saw him saying unto me,* **Make haste, and get thee quickly out of Jerusalem: for they will not receive thy testimony concerning me**. [19] *And I said, Lord, they know that I imprisoned and beat in every synagogue them that believed on thee:* [20] *And when the blood of thy martyr Stephen was shed, I also was standing by, and consenting unto his death, and kept the raiment of them that slew him.* [21] *And he said unto me,* **Depart: for I will send thee far hence unto the Gentiles**." *(Acts 22:17-21)*

Orthodox Doctrine always flows back to Jesus Christ who delivered it according to the will of God (the Father) and authorized it to His apostles who delivered it unmodified to the church.

- *"And* **they continued stedfastly in the apostles' Doctrine** *and fellowship, and in breaking of bread, and in prayers."* (**Acts 2:42**)
- *"Then the deputy, when he saw what was done, believed,* **being astonished at the Doctrine of the Lord**." (**Acts 13:12**)

WE ARE NOT TO RECEIVE ANYONE THAT DOES NOT BRING THE SOUND DOCTRINE OF CHRIST:

- "If there come any unto you, and bring not this Doctrine, receive him not into your house, neither bid him God speed:" (**2 John 1:10**)
- "For **the time will come when they will not endure** sound doctrine; but after their own lusts shall they heap to themselves teachers, having itching ears;" (**2 Timothy 4:3**)
- "For whoremongers, for them that defile themselves with mankind, for menstealers, for liars, for perjured persons, and **if there be any other thing that is contrary to** sound doctrine;" (**1 Timothy 1:10**)

WE ARE INSTRUCTED TO SPEAK THE SOUND DOCTRINE OF CHRIST ACCORDINGLY, AS WE HAVE TAUGHT:

- *"**But speak thou the things which become** sound doctrine:"* (**Titus 2:1**)
- *"Holding fast the faithful word as he hath been taught, that he may be able by sound doctrine both to exhort and to convince the gainsayers."* (**Titus 1:9**)

THE SOUND DOCTRINE OF CHRIST -VERSES- THE DOCTRINE OF MEN AND DEVILS:

- *"That we henceforth be no more children, tossed to and fro, and carried about with every wind of Doctrine, **by the sleight of men**, and cunning craftiness, whereby they lie in wait to deceive;"* (**Ephesians 4:14**)
- *"Now the Spirit speaketh expressly, that in the latter times some **shall depart from the faith**, giving heed to seducing spirits, and Doctrines **of devils**;"* (**1 Timothy 4:1**)
- *"If any man teach otherwise, and **consent not to wholesome words, even the words of our Lord Jesus Christ, and to the** Doctrine **which is according to godliness**;"* (**1 Timothy 6:3**)

GUARD YOUR EYE GATE AND EAR GATE

According to Pastor Myron B. Bulger, 'As believers, it is extremely imperative that we understand the significance of guarding our *eye and ear* gates. Even more so today, because we are in the communication era. Every day we are overwhelmed with a bombardment of *information of various types*. There is music, movies, TV, radio, internet, computers, tablets, smart phones, Tinder, Twitter, and Snapchat just to name a few. Christians must address these types of questions:

- What are we to do with all this information?
- What is the source of this information?
- How are we to process the information?
- Are we conscious of the intended purpose of the content?
- Is both the purpose and source biblical, non-biblical, or anti-God?

We must be vigilant, watchful, and protective of *our eye and ear gates*; they are the window, and pathway to our heart and soul.

> "*The light of the body is the eye: therefore when **thine eye** is single, thy whole body also is full of light; but when thine eye is evil, thy body also is full of darkness.*" (**Luke 11:34**)

Jesus made it very clear as related to controlling the eyes, and the effect it has on us when we don't control the content allowed in through the eye gate.

The Scripture expresses the importance of guarding our hearts by keeping our *eyes and ears* focused on God:

> "*My son, attend to my words; incline **thine ear** unto my sayings. 21 Let them not depart from **thine eyes**; keep them in the midst of thine heart. 22 For they are*

*life unto those that find them, and health to all their flesh. 23 Keep thy heart with all diligence; for out of it are the issues of life. 24 Put away from thee a froward mouth, and perverse lips put far from thee. 25 Let **thine eyes** look right on, and let **thine eyelids** look straight before thee."* (**Proverbs 4:20-25**)

Jesus said:

*"But I say unto you, That whosoever **looketh** on a woman to lust after her hath committed adultery with her already in his heart."* (**Matthew 5:28**)

He is warning us to protect our eye gate. When we give place to things that are not of God, then we fall into sin.

King David found himself in a comparable situation when he looked upon Bath-sheba; instead of guarding his **eye gate**, he gave place to it and sinned against God. After repenting and learning from his failings, he responded:

"I will set no wicked thing before mine eyes: I hate the work of them that turn aside; it shall not cleave to me." (**Psalm 101:3**)

When it comes to the ear gate, I would ask these questions:
- What are your influences?
- What are you listening to?

Our influences, regardless of whether they are *good or bad* affect us:

"Be not deceived: evil communications corrupt good manners." (**1 Corinthians 15:33**)

The positive side of our ear gate and what we listen to is explained in these two passages:

"*14 How then shall they call on him in whom they have not believed? and how shall they believe in him of whom they have not heard? and how shall they hear without a preacher? 15 And how shall they preach, except they be sent? as it is written, How beautiful are the feet of them that preach the gospel of peace, and bring glad tidings of good things! 16 But they have not all obeyed the gospel. For Esaias saith, Lord, who hath believed our report? 17 So then faith cometh by hearing, and hearing by the word of God.*" (**Romans 10:14-17**)

"*3 Blessed is he **that readeth**, and they **that hear** the words of this prophecy, and keep those things which are written therein: for the time is at hand.*" (**Revelation 1:3**)

It is important that we give place to the things of God, and **we must block** things that are contrary to the Word of God.

"*Casting down **imaginations**, and **every high thing that exalteth itself against the knowledge of God**, and bringing into captivity every thought to the obedience of Christ;*" (**2 Corinthians 10:5**)

I exalt the **body of Christ**; let us defend ourselves with the whole armor of God, denying ourselves, and submitting everything unto God. The Apostle James reminds us what would happen if we don't guard our **eye and ear gates** and give place to sin:

"*14 But every man is tempted, when he is drawn away of his own lust, and enticed. 15 Then when lust hath conceived, it bringeth forth sin: and sin, when it is finished, bringeth forth death.*" (**James 1:14-15**)'[53]

Here are a few more eye and ear gate Scriptures:

---

[53] Pastor Myron B. Bulger; Associate Pastor at Strictly Biblical Bible Teaching Ministries.

*"He that planted **the ear**, shall he **not hear**? he that formed **the eye**, shall he **not see**?"* (**Psalms 94:9**)

*"The hearing **ear,** and the seeing **eye**, the Lord hath made even both of them."* (**Proverbs 20:12**)

*"I will set no wicked thing **before mine eyes**: I hate the work of them that turn aside; it shall not cleave to me."* (**Psalms 101:3**)

*"I will **lift up mine eyes** unto the hills, from whence cometh my help. 2 My help cometh from the Lord, which made heaven and earth."* (**Psalms 121:1-2**)

*"Lift up your heads, **O ye gates**; and be ye lift up, ye everlasting doors; and the King of glory shall come in."* (**Psalms 24:7**)

***"The light of the body is the eye**: if therefore thine eye be single, thy whole body shall be full of light."* (**Matthew 6:22**)

Take heed how (Luke 8:18) and what (Mark 4:24) you hear!

MY DOG IS BIGGER THAN YOUR DOG

Christians should avoid the ***"my dog is bigger than your dog"*** or *"**my flesh is better than your flesh**"* mentality. At the end of the day, a dog is a dog and flesh is just flesh. As for me, if it is not about Jesus Christ, then it doesn't matter who and/or what you know. Like Paul:

*"For I determined not to know any thing among you, **save Jesus Christ, and him crucified.**" (**1 Corinthians 2:2**)*

Christians don't have to win the argument, but we do have to be (remain) Biblical. The color of a person's skin is not a Christian Issue, but love is what Christ demonstrated and commands of us (**John 13:34-35**). No, it was not skin color that God had an issue with, but sin, sinners. Sin is not weighed by skin color. Show me the man who plays the absurd game:

- *"**My** sin is bigger than **your** sin"*
- *"**Your** sin is bigger than **my** sin"*
- *"**White** sin is bigger than **Black** sin"*
- "**Black** sin is bigger than **White** sin"

Those views are ridiculous and void of understanding that the "**wages of sin is death**" (**Romans 6:23**). "*My,*" "*Your,*" "*black,*" *and "White*" are all on the same "**second death" boat**, without the saving grace of Jesus Christ.

Apostle Paul instructs and warns:

"*But avoid*
- ***foolish questions**, and*
- ***genealogies**, and*
- ***contentions**, and*
- ***strivings about the law;***
for they are unprofitable and vain." (**Titus 3:9**)

"*Neither give heed to*
- ***fables** and*
- ***endless genealogies,***
  - *which minister questions,*
  - ***rather than godly edifying** which is in faith: so do.*" (**1 Timothy 1:4**)

No one is saved by tracing and trying to prove **bloodlines** through or outside of Scripture. Because of Adam's transgression and now our own (**Romans 5:12-14**), God determined who and what type of atoning sacrifice would be acceptable for the redemption of mankind. It is clear from Scripture:

- God has not hidden what he did, whether we like it or not:

  *"And hath **made of one blood all nations of men**"* **(Acts 17:26-a)**

- God has not hidden why He did it; His intent for all men:

  "*for to dwell on all the face of the earth*," **(Acts 17:26-b)**

- God has not hidden what He predetermined: Skin colors did not catch God by surprise!

  "and hath determined the times before appointed, and the bounds of their habitation;" **(Acts 17:26-c)**

- God has never hidden His heart's desire:

  "That **they should seek the Lord**,
    - if haply **they might feel after him**,
    - and **find him**,
  though he be not far from every one of us:" **(Acts 17:27)**

True followers of Christ never set up barriers and stumbling blocks to hinder others from seeking salvation through the Lord Jesus Christ. They don't attach yokes to the Gospel of Jesus Christ. Salvation was made simple. Why? Because God:

> *"Who **will have all men to be saved**, and **to come unto the knowledge of the truth**. 5 For there is **one God, and one mediator between God and men, the man Christ Jesus**; 6 Who gave himself a ransom for all, to be testified in due time."*
> **(1 Timothy 2:4-6)**

What is it that people don't understand about being
"**Born Again**"? Oh, I know, it's a God thing! You don't
have anything to do with it. Not you, your blood, your
flesh, or your will. God did it, born from above. Just as
you had absolutely nothing to do with your earthly birth.
You didn't get to dictate the color of your eyes, skin,
size, or anything else.

And now over two thousand years later, people want to
change the evidence for salvation. What is it that
groups, such as the so-called Black Hebrew Israelites,
don't comprehend about this Scripture?

> "But **as many** as **received** him,
> - **to them** gave he power to become the sons
>   of God, even
> - **to them** that **believe** on his name:
>
> 13 Which were born,
> - **not of blood,**
> - **nor of the will of the flesh,**
> - **nor of the will of man,**
>
> but of God." (**John 1:12-13**)

ENEMIES OF THE GOSPEL

In the verses below, it is incomprehensible to Paul that
the Galatians could actually be enticed to stoop to
mixing or blending the **Law and grace**. He calls it a
different gospel, thus declaring that mixing law with the
gospel is a **distortion of the truth**.

> "6 I am astonished that you are
> - so quickly **deserting him** who called you in
>   the grace of Christ
> - and are **turning to a different gospel**
>
> 7 not that there is another one,
> - but there are **some who trouble you**
> - and **want to distort the gospel of Christ**.

8 But even if we or an angel from heaven should preach to you **a gospel contrary** to the one we preached to you,

- **let him be accursed.**

9 As we have said before, so now I say again: If anyone is preaching to you **a gospel contrary** to the one you received,

- let him be accursed." (**Galatians 1:6-9**)

In the same sense, today it would be incomprehensible to Paul that the Church could be enticed to call what God called **"evil practices,"** we have turned to calling it *GOOD and wholesome Love*, when God calls it lust (**Romans 1:24**).

Paul would be astonished that we have
- deserted **sound doctrine**
- and deserted **the witness of nature**
- **become fools**, while claiming to be wise (**Romans 1:22**)
- And **have been enticed to distort the truth** that he wrote under the authority of the Holy Spirit (**Romans 1:26-27**:
  - **women exchanged natural relations for those that are contrary to nature;**
  - 27 and **the men likewise gave up natural relations with women** and were **consumed with passion** for one another,
  - **men committing shameless acts with men** and receiving in themselves the due penalty for their error.
- The audacity to marry this abomination in the building that we call **the house of God**, over **the people of God,** and in **the presence of God** calling it love!

According to Paul when dealing with known practices of sin in the Church:
- Such practices *should have been removed far from us* (**1 Corinthians 5:2**)

- Such persons *should have been turned over to Satan* for the destruction of the flesh, so that his spirit may be saved in the day of the Lord. (**1 Corinthians 5:5**)
- **a little leaven leavens the whole lump** (**1 Corinthians 5:6**)

Notice, the above was not a twisting of Scripture: **Practicing Sin** openly was the subject and dealing with it openly was the **Biblical solution**. And we are instructed not to associate with what the Bible calls "**sexually immoral**" people in the church (**1 Corinthians 5:9**). In fact, contrary to popular belief, he argues, isn't it the ones on the inside of the church that **we should be judging** (without being hypocritical)? (**1 Corinthians 5:12**)

Homosexual practices, **just as all practicing sins**, are enemies of the Gospel; just as many of us were before being washed and born again into a new and living way and forsaking the old man, denying ourselves. The problem is unbelief.

God would never overpower their unwillingness to believe and force them to turn to the truth of God.

The **Homosexual excuse** "*I was born that way*" is flawed because we all were born in sin and shaped in iniquity (**Psalms 51:5**). In other words, "**we all were born that way**," and we all must be born again (John 3:7).

It is not enough for the homosexual community to believe the "**Love LIE**":

- o Two Men or of two Women;
- o Two mommies or two daddies.

They want the church to go to hell with them in a breadbasket. Their goal is to promote change to church Biblical doctrine:

- They want to sit in the front rows of the pews with their same-sex partner.
- They want to stand behind the pulpits parading this evil lifestyle as God approved.

It is not the secular world they're concerned about. But they believe that if they can conquer the church, all other dominos fall into place. They attack the church at the core of Jesus teaching "**LOVE**," but not in the doctrinal sense. Rather, they distort the usage of the term "Love," and bind it to the words "*tolerance and intolerance.*"

Jesus instructed: "You have heard that it was said, 'You shall love your neighbor and hate your enemy.' 44 But I say to you, **love your enemies and pray for those who persecute you**," (**Matthew 5:43-44**)

- We are **to pray** for the LGBT community (**Matthew 5:44**):
- We are **to do** good by the LGBT community that hates you (**Luke 6:27**).
- We are **to pray** for the LGBT community who despitefully abuse you (**Luke 6:28**)
- We are **to bless** the LGBT community that curse (speak badly about) you (**Luke 6:28**).
- We are to be merciful to the LGBT community who showed no mercy (**Luke 6:36**).

We learn from Paul (**Romans 12:20-21**):

- if your enemy (the LGBT community) is hungry, feed him;
- if he (the LGBT community) is thirsty, give him something to drink;
- If the enemy (the LGBT community) is wounded, we heal (hospitalize them)

But nowhere in Scripture does it say to "**tolerate the sin of your enemy**" or anyone else in the church.

- o Nowhere in Scripture does it say, **"if the truth offends your enemy, apologize for speaking the truth."**
- o Nowhere in Scripture are we instructed to **"compromise the truth for an enemy, friend, or a loved one."**
- o Nowhere in Scripture are we told, **"turn from following God, but rather turn and follow the understanding of our enemies or anyone else."**

In fact, doing any of these would violate the LOVE that we are to have for God, our Lord and Savior Jesus Christ.

- o We are instructed, "speak the truth in love" (**Ephesians 4:15**).
- o We are instructed "Preach the word; be instant in season, out of season; reprove, rebuke, exhort with all longsuffering and doctrine" (**2 Timothy 4:2**).

The problem is not with how we spoke it, but that we dared to speak (it at all)! Speaking the truth either "to" or "in the presence" of the enemy of the gospel has been declared "**Hate Speech**" by the LGBT community. They have declared war, whether you want to fight or not. They want to pull down our stronghold, which is the Word of God. Welcome to the battle against all practicing of sin. It is not the people with whom we are in battle:

"For we wrestle not against flesh and blood, but against principalities, against powers, against the rulers of the darkness of this world, against spiritual wickedness in high places." (**Ephesians 6:12**)

It is not loving to see people drowning in sin, and not toss them the same lifeline that was thrown to you when you choose to look the other way.

It is not hateful to show a person Biblically that he or she is overtaken by sin. In fact, the exact opposite is true. Sin leads to death (**James 1:15**), and we demonstrate love to the sinner by speaking the truth in love (**Ephesians 4:15**). And, we hate the sin by refusing to condone, ignore, or excuse it.

We are to have compassion on sinners for whom Christ died:

> *"And such were some of you: but ye are washed, but ye are sanctified, but ye are justified in the name of the Lord Jesus, and by the Spirit of our God."*
> (**1 Corinthians 6:11**)

We are also to keep ourselves "from being polluted by the world"—part of what constitutes "pure and faultless" religion:

> *"Pure religion and undefiled before God and the Father is this, To visit the fatherless and widows in their affliction, and to keep himself unspotted from the world."* (**James 1:27**)

"But we also realize that we are imperfect human beings and that the difference between us and God regarding loving and hating is vast. Even as Christians, we cannot love perfectly, nor can we hate perfectly (i.e., without malice). But God can do both perfectly because He is God. God can hate without any sinful intent.

Therefore, He can hate the sin and the sinner in a perfectly holy way and **still lovingly forgive the sinner at the moment of repentance and faith**:"[54]

---

[54] https://www.gotquestions.org/love-sinner-hate-sin.html#ixzz3ea74JGOw (May 16, 2017)

- "And I hated Esau, and laid his mountains and his heritage waste for the dragons of the wilderness." (**Malachi 1:3**)
- "But this thou hast, that thou hatest the deeds of the Nicolaitans, which I also hate." (**Revelation 2:6**)
- "The Lord is not slack concerning his promise, as some men count slackness; but is longsuffering to us-ward, not willing that any should perish, but that all should come to repentance." (**2 Peter 3:9**)

CHAPTER FIVE

CHRISTIANS

BEFORE JOINING A CHURCH:

Before joining a church, ask immediately to see the church doctrinal statement. This is a statement of beliefs. Contrary to popular belief it is not how good the choir sings, how good the preacher can moan and groan with smooth rhetoric, or how friendly the people there seem to be. First on the list is what are the teachings of the church, their beliefs. If you are already a (Biblical) Christian you should already be aware of the **essentials of the faith** and would know if their doctrinal statement lines up with Christian orthodoxy.

Now if you are a new convert, assuming you don't know the Bible, this might be a little rough for you because you are just a learner at this stage. You may not know what to look for in the doctrinal statement. Don't simply go by what the members of the church tell you. Often they are not aware of the church doctrinal statement and what defines **sound doctrine**. The goal of this book is to provide you with insight on what should be looked for and what should be avoided. It is never too late to leave a church that teaches false doctrine. Once you become aware that the church is teaching false doctrine, you should immediately leave that church.

No one will continue to shop at a grocery store that stocks and sells rotten meat no matter how nice the merchant smiles at you: you'll exit quickly. The same thing applies when it comes to your local church. Your loyalty should be to Jesus Christ and whatever helps you to be of service to Him. You can't do that in a church that is teaching false doctrine. Sound Doctrine is essential to the spiritual growth and health of the members of a church. This does not mean that you agree on everything. There can be things in orthodoxy that we differ over but are not divided over. But when it comes down to the main things and the plain things, they are non-negotiable. You will be judged by God based on following truth or following error.

CHURCH BAPTISM:

Church Baptism is essential in the sense of obedience to the gospel. No, the water does not save anyone. Of course, there will be people in heaven that were not baptized in water, for example, the thief on the cross (**Luke 23:39-43; Matthew 27:38, 44**), for there was no way he could get down and be baptized, but:

*"And Jesus said unto him, Verily I say unto thee, **Today shalt thou be with me in paradise.**"* (**Luke 23:43**)

However, baptism is essential in terms of obedience to the gospel when it is possible for a person to obey. But there can be obstacles which prevent a person from obeying. Hence there is no way under their control to take part and be baptized through immersion in the water. In this case, the person wants to comply but is unable to do so.

In the book of Acts, we see the entire process: Philip and the Ethiopian eunuch (**Acts 8:26–39**). Philip preaches the gospel of Jesus Christ to him (vs 35) and the Ethiopian eunuch receives Christ (vs 37) and then Philip baptizes him (vs 38).

So, if you can get baptized, you should. It is the proper symbol of showing your *death, burial, and resurrection with Jesus Christ.* But if you die before that happens and for some reason you could not get baptized, you still go to heaven as a believer in Christ Jesus because you did confess and receive Him as your Lord and Savior (**Romans 10:9-10**).

I will say this as related to whether a person is sprinkled or dunked[55]:

The symbol is Jesus being buried; that is, covered or entombed in something and then coming out. We baptize in water because water symbolizes this.

"Know ye not, that so many of us as were baptized into Jesus Christ were **baptized into his death**? *4 Therefore* **we are buried with him** *by baptism into death: that* **like as Christ was raised up from the dead by the glory of the Father, even so we also should walk in newness of life.** *5 For if we have been planted together in the likeness of his death,* **we shall be also in the likeness of his resurrection:"** **(Romans 6:3-5)**

You are immersed in the water because it is symbolical of your burial or identification with him in death. Coming out of the water is symbolic of the resurrection with him. All Christians should go through this process.[56]

Sprinkling actually came from the early church.[57] They encountered the same thing we encounter today, that there are people that are sick and bedridden. These people could not be brought to any type of baptismal pool to be baptized. The early church having the mindset of performing the baptism as close to what the Biblical symbolism was, they decided it was best to bring the water to these bedridden Christians who could not be immersed and they poured the water or sprinkled it on the bedridden Christians who had accepted Jesus Christ. Of course, God will accept them because this was all they could do. But this does not change the fact that the correct mode of baptism is immersion.

Pastor Moss says, "I have not met a person yet who would not get rebaptized if they thought or felt that

---

[55] http://truthmagazine.com/archives/volume19/TM019182.html (May 5, 2017)
[56] https://apologeticspress.org/apcontent.aspx?category=11&article=1181 (May 5, 2017)
[57] http://www.catholicapologetics.info/apologetics/general/sprinkling.htm (May 5, 2017)

there was something wrong with their baptism. And usually there only two categories of people that talk to me about this subject:

1. People who got baptized so early that they don't know if they really accepted the Lord or not. I advise them that if they have any doubts about it to get baptized again.

2. People who have been sprinkled at either a Methodist Church or Lutheran Church, or Catholic church and/or infant baptism: These are always the ones who have come out of those systems and that want to be baptized again.

No one wants to have to ask the question was my baptism good enough or not? If you feel it wasn't good, then remedy that by getting re-baptized in a way that will increase your faith rather detract from your faith."

BAPTISM OF THE HOLY SPIRIT:

Just because you don't feel something doesn't mean that you didn't get it or don't have it. Being filled is not based on what you feel, but rather what Jesus Christ has done.

Pastor Moss says, *"When I got married over 46 years ago, I didn't feel married. When I said, I Do, **that was it!** I felt the same way. I had to find out what marriage was all about, but from that moment on my life was changing."*

The same thing here with baptism, your salvation is not based on your feelings; whether you shouted, spoke in tongues, etc. It is based upon the fact of what God's Word says. What happens when you are baptized by the Holy Spirit as defined in 1 Corinthian chapter 12:

Spiritual Baptism: When a person gets saved they are placed spiritually into the body of Christ.

> *"For by one Spirit are we all baptized into one body, whether we be Jews or Gentiles, whether we be bond or free; and have been all made to drink into one Spirit."* (**1 Corinthians 12:13**)

The moment you become a believer in Jesus Christ you are placed into the body of Christ. This is *a one-time event* in the life of the believer.

Now on a regular basis in the life of the believer we are filled and renewed daily. Notice the analogy that Paul uses with the "wine" versus "the Holy Spirit" in **Ephesians 5**. We understand what it means to be filled by the Holy Spirit. He controls us, our thought process, mood, actions, and everything else.

> *"18 And be not drunk with wine, wherein is excess; **but be filled with the Spirit**; 19 Speaking to yourselves in psalms and hymns and spiritual songs, singing and making melody in your heart to the Lord; 20 Giving thanks always for all things unto God and the Father in the name of our Lord Jesus Christ;"* (**Ephesians 5:18-20**)

The filling of the Holy Spirit: God, the Holy Spirit, leads you, guides you to teach, to preach, to pray, and to do spiritual work for Him.

Throughout the book of Acts, you see many times when something is done they were filled with the Holy Spirit (**Acts 2:4, 4:8, 4:31, 13:9, 13:52**).

It should be normal for Christians to pray for the filling of the Holy Spirit before we undertake to do anything for the Lord.

CHRISTIAN COMMUNION:

Communion is for believers in Jesus Christ. Not being baptized for whatever valid reason should not stop a believer who has accepted Jesus Christ as their Lord and Savior from receiving Communion.

The accounts of the Lord's Supper are found in the three synoptic gospels and the autoptic gospel (**Matthew 26:26-29; Mark 14:17-25; Luke 22:7-22;** and **John 13:21-30**).

Not found in the Gospels, Apostle Paul writes:

"***For I have received of the Lord that which also I delivered unto you***, *That the Lord Jesus the same night in which he was betrayed took bread: 24 And when he had given thanks, he brake it, and said,*
- *Take, eat: this is my body, which is broken for you:* ***this do in remembrance of me***. *25 After the same manner also he took the cup, when he had supped, saying,*
- *This cup is the new testament in my blood:* ***this do ye***, *as oft as ye drink it,* ***in remembrance of me***. *26*
- *For as often as ye eat this bread, and drink this cup,* ***ye do shew the Lord's death till he come***. *27*
- *Wherefore whosoever shall eat this bread, and drink this cup of the Lord,* ***unworthily, shall be guilty of the body and blood of the Lord***. *28 But* ***let a man examine himself***, *and so let him eat of that bread, and drink of that cup. 29 For*
- ***he that eateth and drinketh unworthily, eateth and drinketh damnation to himself***, *not discerning the Lord's body.*" (**1 Corinthians 11:27-29**).

Verse 26 shows that communion is an essential because of the command: "***this do***" and places a time limit on the communion ceremony until our Lord's return.[58] Anyone that doesn't do communion will have to answer to the Lord Jesus as to why he or she didn't do it. The Lord's Supper/Christian Communion is a remembrance of what Christ did for us and a celebration of what we receive as a result of His sacrifice.

---

[58] https://www.gotquestions.org/communion-Christian.html (May 5, 2017)

CHURCH FELLOWSHIP MANDATORY:

Everything that Christ tells us to do is essential, just like church attendance. It is not a suggestion.

> *"And let us consider one another to provoke unto love and to good works: 25 Not forsaking the assembling of ourselves together, as the manner of some is; but exhorting one another: and so much the more, as ye see the day approaching."* (**Hebrews 10:24-25**)

Often, that is why people are weak in their faith. It is because they didn't fellowship with believers as they were instructed to do.

Jesus tells us to do many things that we don't find out the benefits until later. You can't esteem others or incite others to love and you are missing in action.

Even sinners do this faithfully: they assemble themselves together at the clubs and bars every Friday and Saturday night. Fights don't stop them, shootings don't keep them away, foul language doesn't stop them, being called out of their name doesn't stop them, and the weather doesn't stop them. They park illegally on the sidewalks and on the curbs to get into those places. And often they are the last to leave. Even sinners know the benefit of meeting together with other sinners. But we come up with all types of lame-brain excuses that don't hold water as to why we don't attend church.

> *"It is a fearful thing to fall **into the hands of the living God**."* (**Hebrews 10:31**)

WHAT DEFINES A CHRISTIAN:

What or who defines a Christian? The simple answer is not us! The Bible defines and we simply observe the fruit that grows on trees (including our own tree).

"For a good tree bringeth not forth corrupt fruit; neither doth a corrupt tree bring forth good fruit. 44 For every tree is known by his own fruit. For of thorns men do not gather figs, nor of a bramble bush gather they grapes." (**Luke 6:43-44**)

However, it is not our duty to tell people they are not a Christian, instead, we take them to the Bible. It is God who convicts the heart and draws men to Christ. In the case of a brother or a sister, they might be a backslider. The Scripture says God is married to the backslider (**Jeremiah 3:14**). We warn them, lovingly, and take them to the Bible. It is God who convicts the heart, reproves, and corrects the Christian (**2 Timothy 3:16**).

However, this doesn't mean we look at a pig and call it a possum, or look at an apple and call it an orange. We simply pray the pig will recognize it is a pig and do what a pig does. And we pray the apple should be flushed red, with apple seeds, a black stem, and a green leaf or two attached to the stem. We won't condemn either of them if they don't.   But I will acknowledge that whatever they may be, they don't have the characteristics of any pig or apple that I ever came across.

The word "Christian" is used three times in the New Testament (**Acts 11:26; 26:28; 1 Peter 4:16**). Followers of Jesus Christ were first called "Christians" in Antioch (**Acts 11:26**) because their behavior, activity, and speech were like Christ. The word "Christian" literally means, "belonging to the party of Christ" or a "follower of Christ."

A true Christian is a person who has put faith and trust in the person and work of Jesus Christ, including His death on the cross as the sacrifice for sins and His resurrection on the third day. **John 1:12** tells us, "Yet to all who received him, to those who believed in his name, he gave the right to become children of God." The mark of a true Christian is love for others and obedience to God's Word (**1 John 2:4, 10**). A true Christian is indeed a child of God, a part of God's true family, and one who has been given new life in Jesus Christ.

The Biblical Christian According to the Bible:
1. Abides in the doctrine of Jesus Christ (**2 John 1: 9**).
2. Continues in Jesus's Word (**John 8:30-31**).
3. Will not fellowship with those who pervert, or seek to change the doctrine of Christ (**2 John 1:10-11**).
4. Will take Jesus's Instructions to heart and learn all that the Bible teaches about Jesus (Christology: the Person and His Work) (**Matthew 11:29**).
5. Believes that Jesus is the ONE and only way to the Father to avoid an eternity in hell (**John 14:6**).
6. Is not ashamed of the gospel of Jesus Christ and has no problem assembling with the body of Christ and teaching others the truth of Scripture. They live and wear the label humbly (**Acts 11:26**).
7. Is not a Christian unto him/herself in secret, but out of love and concern seeks to persuade others to become a believer and follower of Jesus Christ (**Acts 26:28**).
8. Understands that they may have to suffer for Christ, to suffer for righteousness' sake due to living, breathing, speaking, sharing, admonishing and teaching the Gospel of Christ, and taking a stand for the inerrancy of Scripture (**1 Peter 4:16**)
9. Understands what it means to be truly religious, having a pure religious lifestyle with integrity and pursuit of holiness according to Scripture (**James1:26-27**).
10. Studies and prepares him/herself to give Biblical answers in Biblical context when asked (**1 Peter 3:15**).
11. Is always ready to defend the faith which was delivered unto the saints (**Jude 3**).
12. Is not **tossed to and fro,** and carried about with every wind of doctrine (**Ephesians 4:14**)
13. Will not accept and/or acknowledge any other gospel, doctrine (**Galatians 1:6**)

14. Will not receive, accept and/or acknowledge anyone who preaches another Jesus whom the Scripture does not authenticate (**2 Corinthians 11: 4**)
15. Believes and defends the 66 books of the Bible and all that they teach.
16. Believes and accepts all that the Bible teaches about Heaven and Hell (**John 5:25, 28-29**; **Revelation 21:1, 8**).
17. Knows how and what to make available and clear to a person who wishes to be saved from eternal damnation. Understands the importance of preaching and witnessing about repentance and remission of sins to all men (**Romans 10:9; Acts 3:19; Acts 2:38; Luke 24:46-47**).
18. Understands that it is the Holy Spirit that enables us and Christ who perfects us. Without Him, we can do nothing (John 14:26; Ephesians 4:12-13; **John 15:5**).

WHY SHOULD I KNOW WHAT THE CULTS TEACH?

Why should a Christian know and study about "cults of Christianity"? if Christians don't, they can unknowingly give allegiance to a false group. Many of these groups come to the house and knock on the new Christian convert's door (and supposedly seasoned Christian's doors) with a Bible in hand. Many of these group's bad theology is infiltrating what should be sound doctrinal churches. Christians must know how to defend the faith:

*"Beloved, when I gave all diligence to write unto you of the common salvation, it was needful for me to write unto you, and exhort you that **ye should earnestly contend for the faith which was once delivered unto the saints**. 4 For **there are certain men crept in unawares, who were before of old ordained to this condemnation, ungodly men, turning the grace of***

our God into lasciviousness, and denying the only Lord God, and our Lord Jesus Christ." **(Jude 3-4)**

Many of them, like the Jehovah Witnesses, know their Bible (New World Translation). They know more about their error than most Christians know about the truth. Dr. Walter Martin said "A trained Jehovah Witness can even mess up a seminary student in about a minute. And it takes less than that with people who are not seminary students because doctrine is not being taught thoroughly today; this is why Christians need to know their Bible." Many of the Jehovah Witness come out of Baptist and Methodist Churches. They were singing, praise dancing, and raising money for the building fund, but they were not learning their Bible. If you don't know Christology, you are meat for the wolves.

There are family members and friends who may now have become enemies of the gospel of Jesus Christ. The Bible speaks of those who left the faith:

"*19* **They went out from us**, *but they were not of us; for* **if they had been of us, they would no doubt have continued with us: but they went out**, *that they might be made manifest that they were not all of us.*" **(1 John 2:19)**

Often, they are in recruit mode. There have been cases where these same people now say that Constantine started Christianity at the Council of Nicea in 325A.D. No doubt they also spout off other unproven claims. Christians should know enough about their Bible to put this false claim to rest within themselves and not be rattled. This can be answered first by internal evidence (Bible) and second, by knowing something about external evidence. Although the Christian should know the answer, it is not your responsibility to give it. You didn't make the claim! Anyone that makes a statement of fact bears the burden of proof.

Ask them what is the evidence for their (bogus) claim. Of course, this is a different approach from teaching or responding to someone that humbly has questions about the Bible and Church History. But you can't give what you don't know. And nobody knows it all! The Christian is ever learning.

> "And if any man **think that he knoweth** any thing, **he knoweth nothing yet as he ought to know**."
> (**1 Corinthians 8:2**)

The bottom line is that a Christian must not only know what he believes and why he believes it but also how to defend what he believes, able to pull others out of the snare and path of the wolves. The Bible provides, instructs, and equips to meet this challenge. But Christians can't defend the Bible if they don't know it.
You are in *Spiritual Warfare:* learn your weapon. You will be (and are) required to know it! Your weapon is not a dust collector.

> "**All scripture is given by inspiration of God**, and is profitable
> * for doctrine,
> * for reproof,
> * for correction,
> * for instruction in righteousness:
> [17] **That the man of God may be perfect, thoroughly furnished unto all good works**." (**2 Timothy 3:16**)

> "**Study to shew thyself approved unto God**, a workman that needeth not to be ashamed, **rightly dividing the word of truth**."(**2 Timothy 2:15**)

You can't use your weapon effectively if you are not familiar with the weapon and have not been trained to use it correctly.

"And Philip ran thither to him, and heard him read the prophet Esaias,
and said, Understandest thou what thou readest? 31
And he said, **How can I, except some man should guide me?"** **(Acts 8:30-31)**

"These were more noble than those in Thessalonica, in that
- **they received the word with all readiness of mind,**
- **and searched the scriptures daily, whether those things were so.**" *(Acts 17:11)*

"Prove all things; hold fast that which is good." **(1 Thessalonians 5:21)**

Paul warns (**Galatians 1:6-9**) that people are going to be preaching another Jesus and another gospel. They may have a Bible in their hand or under the arm. They may even open the Bible, but weigh what comes out of their mouths with the context of Scripture. Yes, it is work being a Biblical Christian and the laborers are few (**Matthew 9:37**)

"For if he that cometh **preacheth another Jesus,** *whom we have not preached, or if ye receive* **another spirit,** *which ye have not received, or* **another gospel,** *which ye have not accepted, ye might well bear with him."* **(2 Corinthians 11:4)**

Jesus instructs the believers to learn of Him (Christology).

"Take my yoke upon you, and **learn of me;** *for I am meek and lowly in heart: and ye shall find rest unto your souls."* **(Matthew 11:29)**

*"**Take heed** unto **thyself**, and unto **the doctrine**; continue in them: for in doing this **thou shalt both save thyself, and them that hear thee.**"* (**1 Timothy 4:16**)

*"**Meditate upon these things**; give thyself wholly to them; **that thy profiting may appear to all**."* (**1 Timothy 4:15**)

MIS-GUIDED CHRISTIANS:

Often people will say the Bible says, "I don't need any man to teach me because I got my Bible and I can read it for myself," referring John's letter; **1 John 2:27**.

*"But the anointing which ye have received of him abideth in you, and **ye need not that any man teach you:** but as the same anointing teacheth you of all things, and is truth, and is no lie, and **even as it hath taught you, ye shall abide in him.**"* (**1 John 2:27**)

They misinterpret the verse. But we know that Scripture interprets Scripture. In the proper perspective and context: John could not in this passage (1 John 2:27) be teaching *"**ye need not that any man teach you.**"*

If John in the passage is teaching *"**ye need not that any man teach you,**"* then he would be contradicting himself. Why? Because John is, in fact, teaching you himself in this letter. Simple logic. This is not what John was talking about. In context, it was what they already knew to be true. Notice:

"23 Whosoever denieth the Son, the same hath not the Father: (but) he that acknowledgeth the Son hath the Father also. 24

- *Let that therefore abide in you, which ye have heard from the beginning.*
- *If that which ye have heard **from the beginning shall remain in you,***

ye also shall continue in the Son, and in the Father." (**1 John 2:23-24**)

John says, never allow anyone to change what you already know to be true. You have been taught the truth so walk in that truth. You don't need any man to teach you the opposite of what you already know to be true. This is what John is teaching in the letter.

Another passage of Scripture we can examine in its futuristic context:

> *"And **they shall teach no more every man his neighbour,***"

> *"*[31] *Behold, the days come, saith the Lord, that **I will make a new covenant with the house of Israel, and with the house of Judah**:*

Notice Jeremiah says the Nation of Israel broke the old covenant, which necessitates a new covenant (**Hebrews 8:13**). The old covenant was no longer in effect and binding, hence a need for a new covenant with the Nation of Israel.

> *"*[33] *But this shall be the covenant that I will make with the house of Israel; After those days, saith the Lord, I will put my law in their inward parts, and write it in their hearts; and will be their God, and they shall be my people. "* (**Jeremiah 31:31-33**)

Notice Jeremiah says this future new covenant with the Nation of Israel shall be the law (law of Christ) written in their hearts and minds (**Hebrews 8:10**).

> *"*[34] *And they shall teach no more every man his neighbour, and every man his brother, saying, Know the Lord: for they shall all know me, from the least of them unto the greatest of them, saith the Lord: for I will forgive their iniquity, and I will remember their sin no more.*[35] *Thus saith the Lord, which giveth the sun*

for a light by day, and the ordinances of the moon and of the stars for a light by night, which divideth the sea when the waves thereof roar; The Lord of hosts is his name: [36] *If those ordinances depart from before me, saith the Lord,* **then the seed of Israel also shall cease from being a nation** *before me for ever."* **(Jeremiah 31:34-36)**

Jeremiah is referring "to after the tribulation period." The Jews will turn back to God and embrace Jesus Christ as their Messiah, then in the Millennial period, the Jews are going to be taught the law and Jesus again. This is what he is referring to when it says, *"they shall teach no more every man his neighbor"* because during the millennium everybody will be learning about the Word of God. Jeremiah is predicting the coming of the New Covenant and what happens *"after that when Israel is restored."* No one will have to ask his neighbor because there will be such widespread teaching taking place.

We know that this is futuristic because it is moving from the old covenant to the new covenant. Jeremiah's focus is on the Jews, viewing them as things will be in the final restoration when they will then be "grafted in" (**Romans 11:24**).

> **"And they shall not teach, each one his neighbor and each one his brother,** *saying, 'Know the Lord,' for they shall all know me, from the least of them to the greatest.* [12] *For I will be merciful toward their iniquities, and I will remember their sins no more."* (**Hebrews 8:10-12** (ESV))

SUFFERING AS A CHRISTIAN:

The new convert (and seasoned Christians) should understand what the Bible says about suffering, important Bible teaching which has been watered down and overshadowed by the pursuit of blessings and material gain in many of today's sermons.

The Bible clearly teaches that Christians are going to suffer. Suffering is a consistent doctrine of the Christian faith. You cannot read through the New Testament without finding suffering mentioned in so many places where it happened. Our Salvation was not free. It cost Jesus His life and every drop of His blood to redeem us. Those that followed Him in obedience lost their lives in service to Him that we might have His gospel in our hands.

Jesus comforts and warns:

> "*These things I have spoken unto you, that in me ye might have peace. **In the world ye shall have tribulation***: *but be of good cheer; I have overcome the world.*" (**John 16:33**)

> "*Blessed are ye, when men shall **revile you**, and **persecute you**, and shall **say all manner of evil against you falsely, for my sake**.*" (**Matthew 5:11**)

In Peter's writings, he discusses suffering. In fact, Peter was writing this to the Church during the time of persecution:

> "*Forasmuch then as Christ hath suffered for us in the flesh, **arm yourselves likewise with the same mind**: for **he that hath suffered in the flesh** hath ceased from sin;*" (**1 Peter 4:1**)

Peter says that suffering brings us closer to God. It shows when you suffer for God. It helps you to be more sanctified and holy.

> "***Yet if any man suffer as a Christian***, *let him not be ashamed; but **let him glorify God on this behalf**.*" (**1 Peter 4:16**)

Paul encourages:

*"29 For unto you it is given in the behalf of Christ, not only to believe on him, **but also to suffer for his sake**;"* **(Philippians 1:29)**

Just as Jesus suffered for us, we will suffer for His name's sake. We don't hear this in churches today because many are not preaching the gospel. Instead, many preach things which tickle the congregation's ears, things that are pleasing to people rather than preaching the truth of the gospel.

Notice in **Acts 14** how certain of the Jews incited the people and stoned Paul for preaching the gospel of Jesus Christ and left him for dead. Even so, Paul and the others returned again preaching the gospel:

*"Confirming the souls of the disciples, and exhorting them to continue in the faith, and that **we must through much tribulation enter into the kingdom of God**."* **(Acts 14:22)**

Suffering and tribulation are, most definitely, part of the Christian faith. These so-called "feel good" and "seeker friendly" churches are bad because they don't tell people the straight-out truth of Scripture, but rather things people want to hear. It is comparable to marketing's supply and demand. There is a demand for "feel-good-messages," and there are many churches ready to meet the supply. But the Scriptures are clear about the subject of suffering, for it is mentioned all through the Bible.

Notice how easy it is to find these passages, assuming you don't skip over them.

Some want to use these verses "by His stripes we are healed" as if just to say that produces a miraculous result for you. But that is not really what the Bible tells us. In fact, the Bible tells us something else. **Romans chapter 8:**

Paul tells us we must suffer with Jesus to be glorified with Him.

> "*17 And if children, then heirs; heirs of God, and joint-heirs with Christ;*
> * *if so be that **we suffer with him**, that*
> * ***we may be also glorified together**.*

Paul says there is suffering in this present time. Yes even today, there is suffering in this present time. People are being slaughtered in other countries for having Bibles in their possession and for identifying with Christ as Christians.

> 18 For I reckon that **the sufferings of this present time are not worthy to be compared with the glory which shall be revealed in us**." (Romans 8:17-28)

Notice the verse above does not say, "you can name-it, claim-it, or speak-it away." But, it causes us to realize that suffering here cannot be compared to the glory which we shall receive afterward.

> "*19 For the earnest expectation of the creature waiteth for the manifestation of the sons of God. 20 For the creature was made subject to vanity, not willingly, but by reason of him who hath subjected the same in hope, 21 Because the creature itself also shall be delivered from the bondage of corruption into the glorious liberty of the children of God. 22 **For we know that the whole creation groaneth and travaileth in pain together until now**. 23 And not only they, but **ourselves also**, which have the firstfruits of the Spirit, even we ourselves groan within ourselves, waiting for the adoption, to wit, the redemption of our body.*" (**Romans 8:19-23**)

Paul is writing to the church; we ourselves are waiting for our bodies to be redeemed. Hard Truth: For as long as you are in a body, you are going to have some pains and experience suffering.

> "24 For we are saved by hope: but hope that is seen is not hope: for what a man seeth, why doth he yet hope for? 25 But if we hope for that we see not, then do we with patience wait for it." (**Romans 8:24-25**)

A *negative or positive confession* will not change the fact that Christians are waiting for new bodies and eternal life in these bodies according to the Scripture. In other words, God can heal us, but we are still going to die (**Hebrews 9:27**).

> "26 Likewise the **Spirit also helpeth our infirmities**: for we know not what we should pray for as we ought: but the Spirit itself maketh intercession for us with groanings which cannot be uttered. 27 And he that searcheth the hearts knoweth what is the mind of the Spirit, because he maketh intercession for the saints according to the will of God." (**Romans 8:26-27**)

Paul says we don't know how to pray. That's why you can't name-it and claim-it. We don't know what to "*name*," and we don't know what to "*claim*." The Holy Spirit is He that intercedes for us at times in our prayers because we don't know how to pray as we should. In this life, we don't have perfect health, even though God heals we are going to die (**Hebrews 9:27**). Sometimes there can be an over expectation on the part of the saints. But God answers prayers according to His will (**1 John 5:14**).

Words like suffering and sin are lost words in many of today's churches. In many cases, these words have been redefined and watered down to make them palatable to the hearers. Many Christians in America are far removed from the reality[59] of rooted teachings within Scripture and the suffering in other countries as related to what the Bible actually teaches.

---

[59] http://www.letusreason.org/Doct13.htm (May 12, 2017)

- **John the Baptist** lost his head. **Matthew 14: 1-12.**
- **Zechariah** murdered - **Matthew 23:35.**
- **Stephen** stoned – **Acts 7:54-60.**
- **James** the brother of John was killed by the Sword. **Acts 12:1-2.**
- **Antipas** faithful servant of God who was murdered. **Revelation 2:12-13.**
- The Two Witnesses that will be murdered during the tribulation period. **Revelations 11:7-8.**
- All of the Apostles (except John and Judas Iscariot) were martyred according to traditional history. [60]
- Others that will be martyred during the tribulation period. **Revelations 6:9-11.**
- Early Church fathers who were martyred for the faith. [61]

Christian Persecution Around The Globe:

- **Article in USATODAY:** "Persecution of Christians isn't rare: Franklin Graham"
  - "It's one thing to destroy a building, but Christians are dying for their faith. And it's not just in Iraq."[62]
- **Article CNN**: "Christian persecution reached a record high in 2015, the report says."
  - "The group's report defines Christian persecution "as any hostility experienced as a result of one's identification with Christ." Open Doors found this persecution ranged from imprisonment, torture, beheadings and rape to the loss of home and assets, the loss of a job, or even rejection from a community."[63]
- **Christianity Today**: "Persecution"

---

[60] http://www.bibleinfo.com/en/questions/who-were-twelve-disciples (May 12, 2017)
[61] https://en.wikipedia.org/wiki/List_of_Christian_martyrs (May 12, 2017)
[62] https://www.usatoday.com/story/opinion/2017/05/07/christian-persecution-world-egypt-iraq-mexico-column/101279550/ (May 12, 2017)
[63] http://www.cnn.com/2016/01/17/world/christian-persecution-2015/ (May 12, 2017)

- o "From verbal harassment to hanging, persecution for professing faith in Christ is as old as Christianity itself, often coming with ethnic violence and geo-political conflict. In the 20th century, Christians in formerly Communist countries went underground with their faith, eventually gaining support and advocacy from missionary Brother Andrew and his Open Doors USA. Today the nonprofit compiles an annual list of the world's worst persecutors of Christians; Muslim countries with stringent Shari'ah law comprise 8 of the top 10 worst."[64]

- **FoxNews**: "Christian persecution seen in more locations across the globe, new report shows"
  - o "In the past year, the persecution of Christians has not only increased, but it has also spread to more corners of the globe – with incidents occurring on every continent, according to a new report."[65]

- **Breitbart:** "Report: 90,000 Christians Killed for Their Faith in 2016"
  - o "During the year 2016, some 90,000 Christians were killed for their faith around the world, according to a new study from the Turin-based Center for Studies on New Religions (CESNUR)."[66]

- **CNSNEWS**: "2011, Christians in Syria 1.25 Million; 2016, Christians in Syria Less Than 500,000"
  - o "It notes that "Christians are the most persecuted religious group in the world" and that in at least 104 countries Christians are

---

[64] http://www.christianitytoday.com/ct/topics/p/persecution/ (May 12, 2017)
[65] http://www.foxnews.com/world/2017/02/02/christian-persecution-seen-in-more-locations-across-globe-new-report-shows.html (May 12, 2017)
[66] http://www.breitbart.com/national-security/2017/01/01/report-90000-christians-killed-faith-2016/ (May 12, 2017)

harassed and persecuted by governments and organizations.

- o The harassment includes "physical assaults, arrests and detentions, the desecration of holy sites and discrimination against religious groups in employment, education or housing," reads the report."[67]
- **Patheos**: "No Persecution?"
  - o 'If you are not being persecuted for your faith in Christ then you are either on a desert island and no one is there to persecute you or you are not living any differently from the world around you…or you are not a Christian at all.
  - o If you are living a godly life you will be persecuted, make no mistake about it, because "all who desire to live a godly life in Christ Jesus will be persecuted" (**2nd Timothy 3:12**).'[68]

Today, in this present time, Christians in America are now being persecuted for practicing their faith. However, there are churches compromising Biblical truth. Intolerance has taken on a new definition with its focus on the church, this means you. Preaching the gospel which calls sin "SIN" has become hate speech, unloving, and intolerant. The Supreme Court has made that which goes against the nature of man lawful. But many churches have forgotten there is a court that is higher than the Supreme Court. This Judge, God, says vengeance is mine. Even so, many churches are falling like dominos.

Why, you might ask in a book that is supposed to be simple and about essentials, would I include a section on suffering? The answer is simple. It's Biblical.

---

[67] http://www.cnsnews.com/news/article/michael-w-chapman/2011-christians-syria-125-million-2016-christians-syria-less-500000 (May 12, 2017)
[68] http://www.patheos.com/blogs/christiancrier/2016/12/26/are-christians-being-persecuted-in-the-united-states/ (May 12, 2017)

> "*I tell you that he will avenge them speedily. Nevertheless when the Son of man cometh, **shall he find faith on the earth**?*" (**Luke 18:8**)

Paul had infirmities:

> "*8 For this thing I besought the Lord thrice, that it might depart from me. 9 And he said unto me, My grace is sufficient for thee: for my strength is made perfect in weakness. Most gladly therefore will I rather glory in my infirmities, that the power of Christ may rest upon me. 10 Therefore I take pleasure in infirmities, in reproaches, in necessities, in persecutions, in distresses for Christ's sake: for when I am weak, then am I strong.*" (**2 Corinthians 12:8-10**)

PERSECUTION ~TO COMPROMISE OR NOT TO COMPROMISE:

The question is what will YOU suffer for His name's sake. It is easy for people to say they won't take the mark of the beast and there is no gun to their head. Yet Christians compromise "simple clear-cut truths" of the Bible today, and we are not in the seven year tribulation period, nor has the Anti-Christ risen up and shown his face.

The Dragon is Satan. He will empower the first beast who is the anti-Christ.

> "*4 And they*
> - ***worshipped the dragon** which gave power unto the beast: and **they***
>   - ○ ***worshipped the beast**, saying,*
>   - ▪ ***Who is like unto the beast?***
>   - • ***who is able to make war with him**?*" (**Revelation 13:4**)

The first Beast is the Anti-Christ. He will empower the second beast who is the false prophet.

"11 And I beheld
- *another beast coming up out of the earth; and he had two horns like a lamb, and he spake as a dragon. 12 And*
- *he exerciseth all the power of the first beast before him, and causeth the earth and them which dwell therein to worship the first beast, whose deadly wound was healed. 13 And*
- *he doeth great wonders, so that he maketh fire come down from heaven on the earth in the sight of men, 14*
- *And deceiveth them that dwell on the earth*
    - *by the means of those miracles which he had power to do in the sight of the beast;*
    - *saying to them that dwell on the earth, that they should make an image to the beast, which had the wound by a sword, and did live. 15 And he had power to give life unto the image of the beast,*
    - *that the image of the beast should both speak, and cause that as many as would not worship the image of the beast should be killed. 16 And*
    - *he causeth all, both small and great, rich and poor, free and bond, to receive a mark in their right hand, or in their foreheads: 17 And that no man might buy or sell, save he that had the mark, or the name of the beast, or the number of his name.*
18 Here is wisdom. Let him that hath understanding count the number of the beast: for it is the number of a man; and his number is Six hundred threescore and six." (**Revelation 13:11-18**)

*"4 And I saw thrones, and they sat upon them, and judgment was given unto them: **and I saw the souls of them that were beheaded for the witness of Jesus, and for the word of God**, and which had not worshipped the beast, neither his image, neither had received his mark upon their foreheads, or in their hands; **and they lived and reigned with Christ a thousand years**."* (Revelation 20:4)

I warn you Biblically not to be as the scoffers who claim to represent Christ, but who, in all actuality, mock the Scriptures with their promoting of "Self Now" disguised as "Kingdom Now." They are quick to say they are not looking for no "pie in the sky" and they have seemingly demoted Jesus Christ to a "rabbit's foot" mentality in the minds of their followers. They practice these deceptions with a smile on their faces. You won't hear them warn and preach about **SIN**, repentance and preparing for the return of Christ.

But Paul says with tears:

*"29 For I know this, that after my departing shall grievous wolves enter in among you, not sparing the flock. 30 Also of your own selves shall men arise, speaking perverse things, to draw away disciples after them. 31 Therefore watch, and remember, that by the space of three years **I ceased not to warn every one night and day with tears**."* (Acts 20:29-31)

*"18 (**For many walk, of whom I have told you often, and now tell you even weeping**, that they are the enemies of the cross of Christ: 19 Whose end is destruction, whose God is their belly, and whose glory is in their shame, who mind earthly things.)"* (Philippians 3:18-19)

Many in the church have turned a deaf ear to what is happening in our country, communities, and neighborhoods, and what has invaded churches that claim to represent Christ. Fearful of losing their 501c status, tithes, and membership, they compromise the truth.

- **FoxNews:** "Christian bakers fined $135,000 for refusing to make wedding cake for lesbians"
  - The Oregon Bureau of Labor and Industry (BOLI) <u>awarded</u> $60,000 to Laurel Bowman-Cryer and $75,000 in damages to Rachel Bowman-Cryer for "emotional suffering."
  - "This case is not about a wedding cake or a marriage," the final order read. "It is about a business's refusal to serve someone because of their sexual orientation. Under Oregon law, that is illegal."[69]
- **Catholic News Agency:** "Christian ministers told to perform gay 'weddings' or face jail time"
  - Boise, Idaho, Oct 20, 2014, / 12:28 pm (CNA/EWTN News).- Two Christian ministers in Coeur d'Alene, Idaho, could face legal punishment or be forced to sell their nearly 100-year-old wedding chapel for declining to perform same-sex "wedding" ceremonies.[70]
- **United Methodist Church:** "Gay couple files complaint for refusal of wedding"
  - 'A United Methodist pastor is facing a complaint under church law because he declined to officiate at a same-sex wedding.
  - The couple, Kenneth Barner and Scott Chappell, charge Carpenter under the

[69] http://www.foxnews.com/opinion/2015/07/03/christian-bakers-fined-135000-for-refusing-to-make-wedding-cake-for-lesbians.html (May 12, 2017)
[70] http://www.catholicnewsagency.com/news/christian-ministers-told-to-perform-gay-weddings-or-face-jail-time-74865/ (May 12, 2017)

Book of Discipline with "failure to perform the work of ministry." Their complaint also accuses Carpenter of "gender discrimination" in not officiating at their ceremony. Gender discrimination is also a chargeable offense under church law.

- o The United Methodist Book of Discipline, the denomination's book of church law and teachings, also states that all people are of sacred worth but the practice of homosexuality is incompatible with Christian teaching." It is a chargeable offense under church law for clergy to preside at same-sex unions.'[71]

- **Lifenews**: "ACLU Loses Lawsuit in Attempt to Force Catholic Hospital to Do Abortions"
  - o "The American Civil Liberties Union (ACLU) is certainly no stranger to clashing with the Catholic Church over its pro-life position. This is especially the case when it comes to Catholic hospitals refusing to perform abortions. A lawsuit from 2013 over such an incident has now been thrown out by a federal judge in Michigan."[72]

- **USA TODAY**: "Presbyterians in U.S. to allow gay marriage ceremonies"
  - o "The Presbyterians are now one of the biggest Christian groups in the U.S. to allow same-sex marriages.
  - o According to Religion News Service, the General Assembly of the Presbyterian Church voted to allow pastors to perform gay marriages wherever they are legal by a vote of 76% to 24%.

- o In two overwhelming votes, the nation's sixth-largest Protestant denomination approved the practice in the 19 states where same-sex marriage is legal and approved presbytery-by-presbytery decisions to change the definition of marriage from a man and a woman to two people."[73]
- **Michigan Chronicle:** excerpt "Michael Nabors, longtime pastor of New Calvary Baptist Church"
  - o Nabors said: "...I am saddened by such a response. I am dismayed by such a response. In fact, my dismay is so strong that in my own way, I recognize my time is far past — to come out of the closet! I am coming out of the closet as a heterosexual, male pastor, with all the privileges this has afforded me in more than 30 years of ministry, to say that I do believe in gay rights. I also believe that if gays love each other in the way I love my wife, in the way that any man-husband loves his woman-wife, it is perfectly fine for them to be married..."[74]
- **Blacdetroit:** "Pastor E.L. Branch of Third New Hope Baptist Church of Detroit."
  - o "**'I support it to the degree that I wonder what's the issue**," says Branch, about the LGBTQ community in the church. "Pastor Nabors is one of our gifted young preachers who I have lots of admiration for, and this only makes me admire him more for his stance on this. The LGBT community is a part of the community of faith and really, to a great degree, always have been."
  - o Last year, **Branch licensed an openly lesbian minister**. And as head pastor of

---

[73] https://www.usatoday.com/story/news/nation/2014/06/19/presbyterians-allow-gay-marriage-ceremonies/10922053/ (May 12, 2017)
[74] https://michronicleonline.com/2015/06/30/black-pastors-in-detroit-grapple-with-gay-marriage-ruling/ (May 12, 2017)

Third New Hope for 37 years, Branch says he can only agree with Nabors' comments, "because it is true." Explaining, he was never taught to be homophobic, but others' behaviors made it clear that it was not acceptable.

- o "I was not taught directly, but indirectly taught that it was wrong to be homosexual," he says, adding, "I was also taught that we are not each other's judges." Branch says his point of "conversion" on the issue was having personal relationships with gay people. '[75]

The references to the churches whose pastors are compromising the faith are not quoted as ad hominem attacks on their person. But we must expose teachings that skew Essentials and the Sound Doctrine of the Christian Faith. There is only one Jesus Christ and only one Gospel of Jesus Christ.

Anything else is counterfeit Doctrine, regardless of how intellectual its promoters may be. Evangelist Anita Campbell points out that telling a person that stores are selling rotten meat, and not to buy it, is useless without telling people which store is selling the rotten meat and warning them not to shop there.

I was angry when I learned someone had passed off a counterfeit twenty-dollar bill to me. It was useless, good for nothing, void. Nor could I in good conscience, knowing it was fake, pass it off to someone else. Instead, I warned people they better be careful. If I would have known who passed it off to me, that would have been a part of the warning. I would have named names!

How much more so when pastors (churches) seek to change the truth of God into a lie (**Romans 3:4**) where

---

[75] http://www.blacdetroit.com/BLAC-Detroit/June-2014/Detroit-Black-Churches-Openly-Accept-Gays-Others-Denounce/ (May 12, 2017)

lives and people's salvation is at stake. We reported no slander but the truth about people boldly proclaimed in interviews. This evidence flowed fearlessly out of their own mouths.

It is not wrong to follow Apostle Paul's example:

"*17 Brethren, be followers together of me, **and mark them which walk so** as ye have us for an ensample.18 (For many walk, of whom I have told you often, and now tell you even weeping, that they are the enemies of the cross of Christ: 19 Whose end is destruction, whose God is their belly, and whose glory is in their shame, who mind earthly things.)*" (**Philippians 3:17-19**)

Here is the list of the 8 evil doers the great apostle was inspired to justifiably identify by name in **2 Timothy**:
- 1) Phygellus [***unloving-turning his back in the time of trouble***] 1:15
- 2) Hermogenes [***unloving-turning his back in the time of trouble***] 1:15
- 3) Hymenaeus [***overthrow the faith of others with error***] 2:17
- 4) Philetus [***overthrow the faith of others with error***] 2:17
- 5) Jannes [***Resisted the truth***] 3:8
- 6) Jambres [***Resisted the truth***] 3:8
- 7) Demas [***apostate – love the world***] 4:10
- 8) Alexander the coppersmith [***withstood the truth and did evil to Paul***] 4:14

John calls out Diotrephes [***who was high-minded and slandered the brethren***] 3 John 1:9

We learn that you will suffer wrong often by those that wear the title "Brother," but God is faithful and renews our strength. Sometimes it is not the leaders but their weak-minded followers who commit the offense against you.

*"22 And when he had thus spoken, **one of the officers which stood by struck Jesus with the palm of his hand, saying, Answerest thou the high priest so**? 23 Jesus answered him, If I have spoken evil, bear witness of the evil: but if well, why smitest thou me?"* (**John 18:22-23**)

*"2 And **the high priest Ananias commanded them that stood by him to smite him on the mouth**. 3 Then said Paul unto him, God shall smite thee, thou whited wall: for sittest thou to judge me after the law, and commandest me to be smitten contrary to the law? 4 **And they that stood by said, Revilest thou God's high priest?**"* (**Acts 23:2-4**)

People do the same today if you speak the truth against their bishops and so-called apostles. It doesn't matter whether it is the truth, they angrily plug-up their ears and strike out at you in defense of their leaders.

But Apostle Paul writes this to the church. If you are not in the Body of Christ, stop up your ears--this is not for you. But if you are in the body take note:

"Now I beseech you, brethren,
- o **mark them which cause divisions and offences**
- o **contrary to the doctrine which ye have learned**;
- o *and **avoid them.***

*18 For they that are such serve not our Lord Jesus Christ, but their own belly; and **by good words and fair speeches deceive the hearts of the simple**."* (**Romans 16:17-18**)

"'Mark them" – the Greek word here for "**mark**" is *skopeo*, which means "to scope out; to take aim at, consider, watch."

Believers are here mandated to wisely scope out closely, observe and scrutinize all teachings and spiritual leaders under the lamp of God's holy Word. We are to closely discern between true and false doctrines and leaders and sound the alarm on that which is found to be inconsistent with holy Writ. This is to be done especially when dealing with foundational, essential truths (which are a salvation issue).

"Therefore I esteem all thy precepts concerning all things to be right; and **I hate every false way**." **Psalms 119:128**'[76]

You may suffer a backlash for warning and for speaking out against the likes of so-called famous leaders whose names are household words. They flood post most of the gospel network channels and radio stations. Their published books like pancakes are stacked right next to the Bibles and Biblical resource material in your neighborhood bookstores.
http://biblefacts.org/pdf/clips.html

- o "'Now this is a shocker! But God has to be given permission to work in this earth realm on behalf of man....Yes! You are in control! So if man has control, who no longer has it? God.....When God gave Adam dominion, that meant God no longer had dominion. So God cannot do anything in this earth unless we let Him. And the way we let Him or give Him permission is through prayer." (Frederick Price Quoted from - "Christianity in Crisis" by H. Hanegraaff, 1993)'[77]
- o Fred Price taught that true Christians don't get sick, audio-A[78] and audio-B[79].
- o Fred Price says if you have to say "thy will be done" it is stupidity and you are calling God a fool, audio-C[80]

[76] http://www.forgottenword.org/naming-names.html (May 12, 2017)
[77] http://www.letusreason.org/Wf27.htm (May 12, 2017)
[78] http://biblefacts.org/pdf/mp3/price-sick4.mp3 (May 12, 2017)
[79] http://biblefacts.org/pdf/mp3/price-sick5.mp3 (May 12, 2017)
[80] http://biblefacts.org/pdf/mp3/thywill.mp3 (May 12, 2017)

- o Fred Price says true Christians are rich, audio-F[81]
- o Kenneth Copeland says God has to have faith rather than him being the object of our faith. Audio-D[82]
- o Kenneth Copeland teaches Adam was a god, audio -E[83]
- o Kenneth Copeland says God was a man that stands about 6'2" and weighs about 200 pounds who stood up and said let it be and the universe situated itself, audio-G[84].
- o Myles Monroe and Benny Hinn say "God needs our Permission," Audio-H[85]

"30 **A wonderful and horrible thing is committed in the land;** 31 The prophets prophesy falsely, and the priests bear rule by their means; and **my people love to have it so**: and what will ye do in the end thereof?" (**Jeremiah 5:30-31**)

"25 *Who changed the truth of God into a lie, and worshipped and served the creature more than the Creator, who is blessed for ever. Amen.*
*26 **For this cause God gave them up unto vile affections***:
- o *for even their **women** did change the natural use into that which is against nature: 27*
- o *And likewise also the **men,** leaving the natural use of the woman, burned in their lust one toward another; men with men working that which is unseemly, and receiving in themselves that recompence of their error which was meet.*
*28 And even as **they did not like to retain God in their knowledge**, God gave them over to a reprobate mind, to do those things which are not convenient; 29 Being filled with all unrighteousness, fornication, wickedness, covetousness,*

---

81 http://biblefacts.org/pdf/mp3/pricerr.mp3 (May 12, 2017)
82 http://biblefacts.org/pdf/mp3/force.mp3 (May 12, 2017)
83 http://biblefacts.org/pdf/mp3/copland-god-man.mp3 (May 12, 2017)
84 http://biblefacts.org/pdf/mp3/6ftman.mp3 (May 12, 2017)
85 https://www.youtube.com/watch?v=c5BDAwnH7SE (May 12, 2017)

*maliciousness; full of envy, murder, debate, deceit, malignity; whisperers, 30 Backbiters, haters of God, despiteful, proud, boasters, inventors of evil things, disobedient to parents, 31 Without understanding, covenantbreakers, without natural affection, implacable, unmerciful: 32 **Who knowing the judgment of God**, that they which commit such things are worthy of death, not only do the same, but have pleasure in them that do them."* (**Romans 1:25-32**; see Leviticus **18:22-24; 20:13**)

Critics love to say that Jesus never said anything about homosexuality. But He did! He referred us to what was acceptable by God. That is a huge statement. Notice, Jesus did not redefine marriage:

*"And he answered and said unto them, Have ye not read, **that he which made them at the beginning made them male and female**, 5 And said,*
- o *For this cause shall **a man** leave father and mother,*
- o *and shall **cleave to his wife**: and*
- o *they twain shall be **one flesh**?*
*6 Wherefore they are no more twain, but one flesh. **What therefore God hath joined together**, let not man put asunder."* (**Matthew 19:4-6**; see **Genesis 2:23-25**)

Apostle Paul upholds this truth by writing to the church:

"Nevertheless, to avoid fornication,
- o *let every **man** have **his** own **wife**, and*
- o *let every **woman** have **her** own **husband**.*
3 Let the husband render unto the wife due benevolence: and likewise also the wife unto the husband." (**1 Corinthians 7:2-3**)

It is not just homosexual practices that are condemned, but any who continue to practice sin and who refuse to repent of these practices:

*"Know ye not that the unrighteous shall not inherit the kingdom of God? Be not deceived: **neither fornicators, nor idolaters, nor adulterers, nor effeminate, nor abusers of themselves with mankind, 10 Nor thieves, nor covetous, nor drunkards, nor revilers, nor extortioners**, shall inherit the kingdom of God. 11 And such were some of you: but ye are washed, but ye are sanctified, but ye are justified in the name of the Lord Jesus, and by the Spirit of our God."*
(**1 Corinthians 6:9-11**)

"12 Wherefore let him that thinketh he standeth take heed lest he fall. 13 There hath no temptation taken you but such as is common to man: but God is faithful, who will not suffer you to be tempted above that ye are able; but will with the temptation also make a way to escape, that ye may be able to bear it." (**1 Corinthians 10:12-13**)

I encourage you not to lose heart and to pray, searching diligently for that which God has already set aside for you. There is a remnant; churches that God has set aside for Himself. Not a perfect people, but the church that abides by the truth of the Word of God and that Church who is willing to suffer for Christ rather than compromise Christian integrity. Join that Church measuring it by every Word of the Scripture. You shop for a car, a suit or a dress, food and pretty much everything else. Yes, today, you must shop for a church, a church where, Biblically, Christ is its head (**Colossians 1:18**). If you have been there twenty years, and the doctrine changes and now contradicts the Word of God, trade that church in for a Sound Doctrinal Church. Your allegiance is not to a building, a pastor, or even people you like. Our allegiance should be to Him with whom we pray to spend eternity.

"If any man come to me, and hate not his father, and mother, and wife, and children, and brethren,

*and sisters, yea, **and his own life also**, he cannot be my disciple."* (**Luke 14:26**)

Clarity:

*"He that **loveth** father or mother **more than** me is not worthy of me: and he that **loveth** son or daughter **more than** me is not worthy of me. 38 And he that taketh not his cross, and followeth after me, is not worthy of me."* (**Matthew 10:37-38**).

CHAPTER SIX

THE LAW:

CHRISTIAN: THE LAW VS GRACE:

There are many who if possible would trouble you as regard to the law. This will require us to ask them what do they mean, why they believe it, and the evidence for believing it as related to the law.

THE ORAL LAW:

The Oral Law is a legal commentary on the Torah, explaining how its commandments are to be carried out. Supposedly, "common sense suggests that some sort of oral tradition was always needed to accompany the Written Law, because the Torah alone, **even with its 613 commandments** [86], is an insufficient guide to Jewish life. For example, the fourth of the Ten Commandments, ordains, "Remember the Sabbath day to make it holy" (**Exodus 20:8**). From the Sabbath's inclusion in the Ten Commandments, it is clear that the Torah regards it as an important holiday. Yet when one looks for the specific Biblical laws regulating how to observe the day, one finds only injunctions against lighting a fire, going away from one's dwelling, cutting down a tree, plowing and harvesting. Would merely refraining from these few activities fulfill the Biblical command to make the Sabbath holy? Indeed, the Sabbath rituals that are most commonly associated with holiness-lighting of candles, reciting the Kiddush [87] (*a blessing recited over wine or grape juice to sanctify*), and the reading of the weekly Torah portion are found not in the Torah, but in the Oral Law.

Without an oral tradition, some of the Torah's laws would be incomprehensible. In the Shema's (prayer) [88] first

---

[86] http://www.jewfaq.org/613.htm (April 28, 2017)
[87] https://en.wikipedia.org/wiki/Kiddush (May 1, 2017)
[88] http://www.dictionary.com/browse/shema (May 1, 2017)

paragraph, the Bible instructs: "And these words which I command you this day shall be upon your heart. And you shall teach them diligently to your children, and you shall talk of them when you sit in your house, when you walk on the road, when you lie down and when you rise up. And you shall bind them for a sign upon your hand, and they shall be for frontlets between your eyes." "Bind them for a sign upon your hand," the last verse instructs. Bind what? The Torah doesn't say. "And they shall be for frontlets between your eyes." What are frontlets? The Hebrew word for frontlets, totafot is used three times in the Torah — always in this context (**Exodus 13:16; Deuteronomy 6:8, 11:18**) — and is as obscure as is the English. Only in the Oral Law do we learn what a Jewish male should bind upon his hand and between his eyes are tefillin (phylacteries).

Finally, an Oral Law was needed to mitigate certain categorical Torah laws that would have caused grave problems if carried out literally. The Written Law, for example, demands an "eye for an eye" (**Exodus 21:24**). Did this imply that if one person accidentally blinded another, he should be blinded in return? That seems to be the Torah's wish. But the Oral Law explains that the verse must be understood as requiring monetary compensation: the value of an eye is what must be paid."[89]

THE DIETARY LAW:

"Kashrut is the body of Jewish law dealing with what foods can and cannot be eaten and how those foods must be prepared. The word "Kashrut" comes from the Hebrew meaning fit, proper or correct.

The word "kosher," which describes food that meets the standards of kashrut, is also often used to describe ritual objects that are made in accordance with Jewish law and are fit for ritual use. Food that is not kosher is referred to as treif (literally torn).

The short answer to why Jews observe these laws is because the Torah says so. The Torah does not specify a reason for these laws but for an observant Jew there is no need for a reason - Jews show their belief and obedience to God by following the laws even though they do not know the specific reason.

In the book *To Be a Jew*, Rabbi Hayim Halevy Donin suggests that kashrut laws are designed as a call to holiness. The ability to distinguish between right and wrong, good and evil, pure and defiled, the sacred and the profane, is very important in Judaism. Imposing rules on what you can and cannot eat ingrains that kind of self control. In addition, it elevates the simple act of eating into a religious ritual. The Jewish dinner table is often compared to the Temple altar in rabbinic literature.

Animals That Cannot be Eaten

Of the "beasts of the earth" (**Leviticus 11:3; Deuteronomy 14:6**).

Of the things that are in the waters, (**Leviticus 11:9; Deuteronomy 14:9**).

The Torah lists forbidden birds (**Leviticus 11:13-19; Deut. 14:11-18**), but does not specify why these particular birds are forbidden.

Rodents, reptiles, amphibians, and insects (**Leviticus 11:29-30, 42-43**).

Kosher Slaughter (Shechitah)

The mammals and birds that may be eaten must be slaughtered in accordance with Jewish law. (**Deuteronomy 12:21**). We may not eat animals that died of natural causes (**Deuteronomy 14:21**) or that were killed by other animals. In addition, the animal must have no disease or flaws in the organs at the time of slaughter. These restrictions do not apply to fish; only to the flocks and herds (**Numbers 11:22**).

Ritual slaughter is known as shechitah, and the person who performs the slaughter is called a shochet, both from the Hebrew root Shin-Chet-Tav, meaning to destroy or kill. The method of slaughter is a quick, deep stroke across the throat with a perfectly sharp blade with no nicks or unevenness. This method is painless, causes unconsciousness within two seconds, and is widely recognized as the most humane method of slaughter possible.

Another advantage of shechitah is that ensures rapid, complete draining of the blood, which is also necessary to render the meat kosher.

The shochet is not simply a butcher; he must be a pious man, well-trained in Jewish law, particularly as it relates to kashrut. In smaller, more remote communities, the rabbi and the shochet were often the same person."

But then there is Christ:

*"On the morrow, as they went on their journey, and drew nigh unto the city, Peter went up upon the housetop to pray about the sixth hour: 10 And **he became very hungry, and would have eaten**: but while they made ready, he fell into a trance, 11*

- *And saw heaven opened, and a certain vessel descending unto him, as it had been a great sheet knit at the four corners, and let down to the earth: 12*

- ***Wherein were all manner of***
  - *fourfooted beasts of the earth,*
  - *and wild beasts,*
  - *and creeping things,*
  - *and fowls of the air. 13*
- *And there came a voice to him,* ***Rise, Peter; kill, and eat****. 14*
- *But Peter said, Not so, Lord; for* ***I have never eaten any thing that is common or unclean****. 15 And*
- *the voice spake unto him again the second time,* ***What God hath cleansed, that call not thou common****. 16*
- *This was done thrice: and the vessel was received up again into heaven."* (**Acts 10:9-16**)

"***For every creature of God is good****, and nothing to be refused, if it be received with thanksgiving:"* (**1 Timothy 4:4**)

"*Him that is weak in the faith receive ye, but not to doubtful disputations. 2 For one believeth that he may eat all things: another, who is weak, eateth herbs. 3 Let not him that eateth despise him that eateth not; and let not him which eateth not judge him that eateth:* ***for God hath received him****.*" (**Romans 14:1-3**)

THE LAW VS FAITH:

The works of the law were the attempts of the Jews to think that salvation could be obtained by the keeping of the law. They are ignorant of God's righteousness and seek to establish their own righteousness by overlooking the fact that Christ is the end of the law described by Moses.

In Romans 10:3-13 Paul contrasts **law** and **faith**:

- the righteousness which is of the law
  - debtor to keep the whole law and live by it.
- the righteousness which is of faith
  - Acknowledge **Christ is the end of the law (10:4)**. **He did what we could not do**. Christ fulfilled the righteousness of the law (**Matthew 5:17**).
  - **Confess Jesus Christ with the mouth** and **believe with the heart**.
  - **Call** on Christ (**Romans 10:13**), **live** in Christ (**Philippians 1:21**), **Walk** in Christ (**Colossians 2:6**).

However, we are not lawless, but rather under the law of Christ.

> "*Brethren, if a man be overtaken in a fault, ye which are spiritual, restore such an one in the spirit of meekness; considering **thyself, lest thou also be tempted**. 2 Bear ye one another's burdens, and so **fulfil the law of Christ**.*" (**Galatians 6:1-2**)

> "*A new commandment I give unto you, That ye love one another; as I have loved you, that ye also love one another.*" (**John 13:34**)

We are under **the law of Christ**[90], understanding He did for us what the Old Testament could not do. But the Old Testament did its job:
- of pointing us to Christ.
- Continuously pointing out our sins which should lead us to Christ.

The Purpose of the Law:

> "*What shall we say then? Is the law sin? God forbid. Nay, I had not known sin, **but by the***

---

90 http://www.biblestudytools.com/dictionaries/bakers-evangelical-dictionary/law-of-christ.html (May 15, 2017)

*law: for I had not known lust, **except the law
had said**, Thou shalt not covet. 8   But sin,
taking occasion by the commandment, wrought
in me all manner of concupiscence. **For
without the law sin was dead**.*" **(Romans 7:7-
8)**

Keeping the Law could never save:

"Is the law then against the promises of God?
God forbid: **for if there had been a law given
which could have given life**, verily
righteousness should have been by the law."
(Galatians 3:21)

"*But when the fulness of the time was come,
God sent forth his Son, made of a woman,
made under the law, 5 **To redeem them that
were under the law**, that we might receive the
adoption of sons.*" **(Galatians 4:4-5)**

**Christ did what the righteousness of the Law
could never do:**

"*2 For **the law of the Spirit of life in Christ
Jesus** hath made me free from the law of sin
and death. 3*
- *For **what the law could not do,** in that it
was weak through the flesh,*
- *****God sending his own Son** in the likeness
of sinful flesh, and for sin, **condemned sin
in the flesh**: 4*
- *****That the righteousness of the law might
be fulfilled in us**, who walk*
  - *not after the flesh,*
  - *but **after the Spirit**.*" **(Romans 8:2-4)**.

God gave Israel **a single law** which included
the Ten Commandments.

[**2 Chronicles 31:3** ....as it is written in the law of the Lord..]

[**Nehemiah 8:2, 3, 8** ...the people were attentive unto **the book of the law**]

[**Nehemiah 8:14,15,18** .... And **they found written in the law** which the Lord had commanded by Moses, that the children of Israel should dwell in booths in the feast of the seventh month:...]

[**Psalms 19:7 The law of the Lord** is perfect, converting the soul:....]

a. The Ten Commandments **were given to the Israelites at Sinai (Exodus 20:1-17)**.
b. Israel was commanded to **obey the Law of Moses**; the law included **the Ten Commandments**.
[**Malachi 4:4 Remember ye the law of Moses** my servant, which **I commanded** unto him in Horeb for all Israel, with the **statutes** and **judgments**.]
   i. Someone keeping one part of the law **must keep the whole law**.

   " *For as many as are of the works of the law are under the curse:*
   for it is written,
   • *Cursed is every one that **continueth not in all things which are written in the book of the law to do them**.*" (**Galatians** 3:10).

   ii. Someone keeping the Ten Commandments **must keep the entire Mosaic Law**.

*"Behold, I Paul say unto you, that if ye be circumcised, **Christ shall profit you nothing.** 3 For I testify again to every man that is circumcised,*

- *that he is a debtor to do the whole law.* 4

- ***Christ is become of no effect unto you,***

*whosoever of you are justified by the law; **ye are fallen from grace**."* **(Galatians 5:2-4)**

c. No one is justified by the works of the law.

Jesus said, *"For verily I say unto you, Till heaven and earth pass**, one jot or one tittle shall in no wise pass from the law, till all be fulfilled."** **(Matthew 5:18)**

The BAD News:

Neither the Jews nor the Gentiles could keep the law or fulfill the law.

The GOOD News:

*"But the scripture hath concluded **all under sin**, that the promise by faith of Jesus Christ might be **given to them that believe.** 23 **But before faith came**, we were kept under the law, shut up **unto the faith which should afterwards be revealed**."* **(Galatians 3:22-23)**

a. **Jesus** came to **fulfill the law.**
*"Think not that I am come to destroy the law, or the prophets: I am not come to destroy, **but to fulfil**."* **(Matthew 5:17)**

b. **Christ is the end of the law** for righteousness to everyone who believes (**Romans 10:4**).

c. Christ is the end of the law because he nailed it to the cross (**Colossians 2:11-14**)

d. Since Jesus fulfilled the law, we can be saved in Christ

- *"**Neither is there salvation in any other**: for there **is none other name under heaven** given among men, **whereby we must be saved**." (**Acts 4:12**)*

- *"**Being justified freely by his grace** through the redemption that is in Christ Jesus:" (**Romans 3:24**)*

- *"Know ye not, **that so many of us as were baptized into Jesus Christ** were baptized into his death?" (**Romans 6:3**)*

- *"For as many of you as have been baptized into Christ have **put on Christ**." (**Galatians 3:27**)*

- *"Thou therefore, my son, **be strong in the grace that is in Christ Jesus**." (**2 Timothy 2:1, 10**)*

e. Now we can walk according to the Spirit

*"There is therefore now no condemnation to them which are in Christ Jesus, who walk not after the flesh, **but after the Spirit**. 2*

- *For the law of the Spirit of life in Christ Jesus hath made me free from the law of sin and death. 3*

- *For what the law could not do, in that it was weak through the flesh,*

- *God sending his own Son in the likeness of sinful flesh, and for sin, condemned sin in the flesh:*
- ⁴ *That the righteousness of the law might be fulfilled in us, who walk not after the flesh, but after the Spirit.*" **(Romans 8:1-4)**

f. Anyone attempting to be justified by law **has fallen from grace.**(Galatians 5:4).

g. The **law was a tutor** (schoolmaster). **Since faith has come, we are no longer under the tutor** (i.e., we are no longer under the law). (**Galatians 3:24-25**).

h. The commandments that were written on stone (i.e., **the Ten Commandments**) brought death. Today we must obey the epistle of Christ which is written on our hearts (**2 Corinthians 3:7-11**).

i. The law was changed. We no longer live under the Ten Commandments or any other part of the Mosaic Law.

*"For **the priesthood being changed**, there is made of necessity **a change also of the law**."* (**Hebrews 7:12**)

God does not change in his nature. He is omnipotent, omniscient, and omnipresent. But God's actions do change.

- In the Old Testament, there was animal sacrifice, but not in the New Testament.
- In the Old Testament, there is a priesthood, but not in the New Testament in the same sense.

God can change His plans, but that does not mean it changes who He is. He is still the same loving and merciful God, full of judgment as it says in **Exodus 34**. He says, "*I change not*" (**Malachi 3:6**). But definitely, He changes in His dispensations and in the fulfillment of His plans.

We see a change as it relates to the Sabbath (which was a part of the Ten Commandments). However, the Sabbath is also fulfilled.   See section on Sabbath.

j. Jesus could not be our High Priest **until God changed the law (Hebrews 7:12-15, 8:4)**

k. Christ came to earth to take away the first covenant (law) and establish the second covenant (law).

> "*Above when he said, Sacrifice and offering and burnt offerings and offering for sin thou wouldest not, neither hadst pleasure therein; **which are offered by the law**; 9 Then said he, **Lo, I come to do thy will, O God. He taketh away the first, that he may establish the second**. 10   By the which will we are sanctified through the offering of the body of Jesus Christ once for all.*" (**Hebrews 10:8-10**)

Apostle Paul writes:

> "*5 Now **the end of the commandment is charity** out of a pure heart, and of a good conscience, and of faith unfeigned: 6 From which some having swerved have turned aside unto vain jangling; 7 **Desiring to be teachers of the law; understanding***

> *neither what they say, nor whereof they affirm.* (**1 Timothy 1:4-11**)

Jesus said:

> "*On these two commandments hang all the law and the prophets.*" (**Matthew 22:40**)
>
> 1) Love God. (**Matthew 22:37-38**)
>
>   - Commandments **1 thru 4**.
>
> 2) Love thy neighbor (others). (**Matthew 22:39**)
>
>   - Commandments **5 thru 10**.

There is no law that can force you to do these. The law only condemns you for failing to keep them. The law says you need a savior and points you to Jesus Christ. The law caused you to realize that you must be born again.

Jesus said and demonstrated what the law could not. The law could not forgive or love, so it could never demonstrate forgiveness or loving another. For the Christian, what was written on tablets of stone, Christ writes these in our hearts[91].

> "*A new commandment I give unto you*,
>
> - *That ye love one another;*
> - *as I have loved you,*
> - *that ye also love one another.*
>
> *35 By this shall all men know that ye are my disciples, if ye have love one to another.*" (**John 13:34-35**)

---

[91] http://thelawofchrist.info/index_files/Comparison_of_Law_of_Moses_with_Law_of_Christ.htm (May 15, 2017)

There is an old saying, misery loves company. People want to put a yoke on the necks of others that they can't carry themselves. Why on earth would anyone consider returning to that which Christ has redeemed us from? And in the face of so many Scriptures, why would anyone consider following the want-to-be law keepers? What if they are wrong? You can't serve two masters: the law and Christ.

Of course, as Christians we submit ourselves to the law of Christ, acknowledging that God did not change his mind about sin and that grace is not a license to sin. That is ludicrous to imply such foolishness and shows one's lack of sound doctrine. Apostle Paul responds:

- o *"What then? shall we sin, because we are not under the law, but under grace?* **God forbid.**" **(Romans 6:15)**

- o *"For **if we sin wilfully after that we have received the knowledge of the truth**, there remaineth no more sacrifice for sins, 27 But a certain fearful looking for of judgment and fiery indignation, which shall devour the adversaries. 28 He that despised Moses' law died without mercy under two or three witnesses: 29 **Of how much sorer punishment, suppose ye, shall he be thought worthy, who hath trodden under foot the Son of God**, and hath counted the blood of the covenant, wherewith he was sanctified, an unholy thing, and hath done despite unto the Spirit of grace? 30 For we know him that hath said, Vengeance belongeth unto me, I will recompense, saith the Lord. And again, The Lord shall judge his people. 31 **It is a fearful thing to fall into the hands of the living God**."* **(Hebrews 10:26-31**"

The Law:

	The Old Covenant. 10 Commandments. (Done away, nailed to the cross)	The New Covenant. The Law of Christ.
1	No other gods beside me.	Brought forward into New Covenant (**I Thess. 1:9**).'Ye turned to God from idols to **serve** the living & true God
2	No graven images.	Brought forward into New Covenant (**Galatians 5:20**). 'works of flesh . . . idolatory.'
3	Don't take God's name in vain.	Brought forward into New Covenant (**I Timothy 1:20**). 'That they may learn not to blaspheme.'
4	Six days shall you work, but the 7th day is the Sabbath.	**Still nailed to the cross (Colossians 2:14-17). Never brought forward. No NT command to keep Sabbath. We rest in Jesus Christ.**
5	Honour your father and mother.	Brought forward into New Covenant (**Ephesians 6:1-3**). 'Honour thy father and mother.'
6	Don't kill.	Brought forward into New Covenant. (**Galatians 5:21**). 'Works of flesh . . . murders.'
7	Don't commit adultery.	Brought forward into New Covenant. (**Galatians 5:19**). 'works of flesh . . . adultery.'
8	Don't steal.	Brought forward into New Covenant. (**Ephesians 4:28**). 'Let him that stole steal no more, let him work to **give**.'
9	Don't bear false witness.	Brought forward into New Covenant. (**Ephesian 4:25**). 'Putting away lying, speak every man the **truth**.'
10	Don't covet.	Brought forward into New Covenant. (**Ephesians 5:5**). 'Nor covetous man who is an idolator.'

In Summary, "The Ten Commandments were essentially **a summary of the entire Old Testament law**. Nine of the Ten Commandments are clearly repeated in the New Testament (all except the command to observe the Sabbath day). Obviously, if we are loving God, we will not be worshipping false gods or bowing down before idols. If we are loving our neighbors, we will not be murdering them, lying to them, committing adultery against them, or coveting what belongs to them. The purpose of the Old Testament law is to convict people of our inability to keep the law and point us to our need for Jesus Christ as Savior (Romans 7:7-9; Galatians 3:24) The Old Testament law was never intended by God to be the universal law for all people for all of time."[92]

92 https://www.gotquestions.org/Crihstian-law.html (May 15, 2017)

SABBATH VS SUNDAY:

The Seventh-Day Adventists ask how can you keep all nine of the ten commandments, but not the 4th commandment?

"*Remember the sabbath day, to keep it holy.*" (**Exodus 20:8**)

What they and other groups such as the Black Hebrew Israelites (BHI), Gathering of Christ Church (GOCC), etc. don't understand is that Christians do keep the Sabbath. But there is something said about the Sabbath day that is not said about any of the other nine commandments that are given to us in the Decalogue (Ten Commandments). Notice in Exodus chapter 31:

"*15 Six days may work be done; **but in the seventh is the sabbath of rest, holy to the Lord: whosoever doeth any work in the sabbath day, he shall surely be put to death.***"

Notice it does **not say** the "**Church**" in verse 16.

"*16 Wherefore **the children of Israel** shall keep the sabbath, to observe the sabbath throughout their generations, for a perpetual covenant.*"

Notice in verse 17 the Sabbath is called **a sign**:

"*17 **It is a sign between me** and **the children of Israel** for ever: for in six days the Lord made heaven and earth, and on the seventh day he rested, and was refreshed.*" (**Exodus 31:15-17**)

Notice what is not called **a sign in Scripture**:

- "Thou shall have no other gods before me" is not called a sign.

- "Thou shall not make unto thee any graven image" is not called a sign.
- "Thou shall not take the name Lord thy God in vain" is not called a sign.
- "Honor thy father and mother" is not called a sign.
- "Thou shall not kill" is not called a sign.
- "Thou shall not commit adultery" is not called a sign.
- "Thou shall not steal" is not called a sign.
- "Thou shall not bear false witness" is not called a sign.
- "Thou shall not covet" is not called a sign.

What does a sign do? A sign points to something. The Sabbath is very important and it is a sign that pointed to Christ. The rest in the Old Testament was a physical rest, but it pointed to the ultimate rest which we have in Christ Jesus. In other words, Jesus Christ is the fulfillment of the Sabbath.

> "**Let no man therefore judge you** in meat, or in drink, **or in respect of an holyday, or of the new moon, or of the sabbath days**: 17 **Which are a shadow of things to come; but the body is of Christ**." (**Colossians 2:16-17**)

Jesus Christ fulfilled the Sabbath day law. Our rest used to be in a day, now it is in Jesus Christ. That is why Apostle Paul could write as he did in Romans chapter 14. Paul would never have written like this if it were not so, being a Pharisee and one (Saul) who knew, practiced, and upheld the law.

> "Who art thou that judgest another man's servant? to his own master he standeth or falleth. Yea, he shall be holden up: for God is able to make him stand. 5 One man esteemeth one day above another: another esteemeth every day alike. **Let every man be fully**

persuaded in his own mind. 6 He that regardeth the day, regardeth it unto the Lord; and he that regardeth not the day, to the Lord he doth not regard it." (**Romans 14:4-6**)

Apostle Paul was a Pharisee who knew all about the Sabbath day. He knew about the Oral Laws that had people doing things on the Sabbath day that the Scripture never commanded. For Apostle Paul to say, let every man be fully persuaded in his own mind means there has been a fulfillment of the law.

There is nothing wrong if a person wants to worship on the Sabbath day, it is fine. There is nothing forbidding one from worshipping on Saturday, Sunday, or any other day. But we can't condemn someone else for choosing to worship on a different day. Sunday worship came about in the early church because Jesus rose from the dead on Sunday: on the eighth day he appeared again to the disciples.

- *"**The first day of the week** cometh Mary Magdalene early, when it was yet dark, unto the sepulchre, and seeth the stone taken away from the sepulchre."* (**John 20:1**)

- *"18 Mary Magdalene came and told the disciples that she had seen the Lord, and that he had spoken these things unto her. 19 **Then the same day at evening, being the first day of the week**, when the doors were shut where the disciples were assembled for fear of the Jews, came Jesus and stood in the midst, and saith unto them, Peace be unto you."* (**John 20:18-19**)

- *"**And after eight days again his disciples were within**, and Thomas with them: then came Jesus, the doors being shut, and stood in the midst, and said, Peace be unto you."* (**John 20:26**)

The Law:

- "**And upon the first day of the week**, when the disciples came together to break bread, Paul preached unto them, ready to depart on the morrow; and continued his speech until midnight." (**Acts 20:7**)

The disciples were not commanded to worship on Sunday, but ever since then, the church has been worshipping on Sunday because Jesus rose on Sunday. But you are free to worship on any day you may choose.

The unbiblical problem is that you have groups like the Seventh-Day Adventists [93] who condemn Christians. They say that when the tribulation begins (not now) that if Christians are still worshipping on Sundays that we are going to get the mark of the beast. This is their teaching under Ellen G. White[94]. A person can read the book of Revelation until the cows come home, but you won't find anything like that there!

Last, but not least; true worship is not based on a place or a day of the week.

*"But the hour cometh, and now is, when **the true worshippers shall worship the Father in spirit and in truth**: for the Father seeketh such to worship him.* [24] *God is a Spirit: and **they that worship him must worship him in spirit and in truth**."* (**John 4:23-24**)

---

[93] http://www.bible.ca/7-mark-beast.htm (April 28, 2017)
[94] http://www.ellenwhite.info/books/ellen-g-white-book-early-writings-ew-15.htm (April 28, 2017)

CHAPTER SEVEN

TRINITY

BIBLICAL TRINITY CONCEPT[95]:

Clearly, when the Bible speaks of **Father**, **Son**, and **Holy Spirit** the Bible is, *in fact, **speaking of three persons*** rather than one. A simple and honest reading (**exegesis**) of the text of Scripture clearly presents three distinct persons. We have numerous verses which indicate ***communication*** and ***relationship*** between persons; such as when Jesus prayed to his Father and the Holy Spirit descended upon him. In other words, since the common sense plain reading of the text indicates three distinct persons, the burden of proof is without a doubt on any group that rejects the doctrine of the Trinity to show the common sense plain reading is false. The Trinitarian does not have the burden of proof. *[paraphrased]*[96]

BRIEF HISTORY ON THE TRINITY[97]:

The doctrine of the Trinity was formally developed in the early church in reaction to errant teaching on the nature of God as found in Arianism.

- Arianism attempted to protect monotheism (the belief in one God) *by denying the full deity of Jesus*, a belief most Christians held at this time.
- Arianism taught that Jesus was divine, **but that he was a lesser deity than the Father.**

To affirm the Church's stance on the nature of God, the Trinity was formally stated in the Nicene Creed (325 A.D.) and the later Athanasian Creed. As a result of these early ecumenical creeds, any departure from the Christian doctrine of the Trinity was considered

---

[95] http://www.theopedia.com/trinity (April 9, 2017)
[96] http://www.apologeticsindex.org/2773-oneness-pentecostalism (April 7, 2017)
[97] http://www.theopedia.com/trinity (April 9, 2017)

heresy. These creeds affirm the early Christian conviction that Jesus was God.

- Arianism caused the church to dogmatically **affirm what was already believed and inherent in the earliest of Christian theology**.

The term "Trinity" is not found in the Bible.
Theophilus of Antioch around 180 A.D. first used the Greek term trias (a set of three) in reference to God, his Word, and his Wisdom.

However, **Tertullian in 215 A.D**. was the first one to state this doctrine using the Latin term, Trinitas (Trinity), referring to the Father, Son, and Holy Spirit (W. Fulton in the *Encyclopedia of Religion and Ethics*).

TRINITY & TRI-UNITY:

Usage:

Trinity: *A group or set of three people or things*

Tri-unity: The fact or state of being three in one (usually with reference to the Christian idea of the Trinity).

Keep in mind when studying this subject that the word "**Trinity**" is not found in Scripture.

This is a term that is used to attempt to describe the triune God—three coexistent, **co-eternal Persons who make up the Godhead**.

WHAT IS THE TRINITY?

The **Trinity** is **the Christian doctrine** that deals with and describes **the nature of God**. The doctrine asserts the following:

- There is one and **only one God**.

- God eternally exists in **three distinct persons**.
- The **Father** is God, the **Son** is God, and the **Holy Spirit** is God.
- The Father **is not** the Son, the Son **is not** the Father, the Father **is not** the Spirit, etc.

THE TRI-UNITY:

Definitions and Distinction:

A. **Unity**--There **are not** two or more gods.
B. **Simplicity**--There **are not** two or more parts in God.
C. **Tri-unity**--There are **three distinct persons** in the one God.

THE TRINITY:

There is
One Divine Being
who coexists eternally
as
three distinct persons
(Father, Son, and Holy Spirit)

TRINITY RELATIONSHIP:

They speak to one another, love one another.

There is a personal relationship **among these three persons**.

The signification of understanding the Trinity is
- The God who made the universe is

  - The same God who came to redeem us from our sins in the person of Jesus Christ and is

- The same God who indwells the believer in the person of the Holy Spirit so that God is totally responsible for our existence and our salvation.

THE DOCTRINE OF THE TRINITY:

The doctrine of the Trinity upholds the following fact:
- it is God who made us,
- it is God who redeems us,
- it is God who is coming back for us.

ONE GOD, that is the Biblical view.

THERE IS ONLY ONE GOD:

The Bible clearly teaches there is only one God. There is **never a deviation** from the fact that there **is but one God**:

- "Hear, O Israel: The Lord our God **is one Lord:**" (**Deuteronomy 6:4**)

- "..that ye may know and believe me, and understand that I am he: before me **there was no God formed, neither shall there be after me.**" (**Isaiah 43:10**)

- "6 ...; **I am the first**, and **I am the last**; and beside me **there is no God**. ...." "8 ... Is there a God beside me? yea, **there is no God**; I know not any.." (**Isaiah 44**)

- "....that they might know thee **the only true God**, and Jesus Christ, whom thou has sent." (**John 17:3**)

- "....**there is none other God but one**. ....6 But to us **there is but one God**, the Father, of whom are all things, and we in him; and one Lord Jesus Christ, by whom are all things, and we by him." (**1 Corinthians 8:4**)

- "Thou believest that **there is one God**; thou doest well: the devils also believe, and tremble." (**James 2:19**)

DEFINITION OF THE TRINITY:

Trinity: Webster's dictionary gives the following definition of trinity:
"The union of **three divine persons** (or hypostases), the **Father, Son,** and **Holy Spirit,** in one divinity, so that all the three are one God as to substance, but three Persons (or hypostases as to individuality)."

Synonyms sometimes used are **triunity**, trine, triality.

The term "trinity" is formed from "tri," three, and "nity," unity.

Triunity is a better term than "**trinity**" because it better expresses the idea of three in one. God is three in one. Hypostases is the plural of hypostasis which means "the substance, the underlying reality, or essence."

"Within the one Being that is God, **there exists eternally three coequal persons**, namely, the Father, the Son, and the Holy Spirit." (TFT, p. 26)

They are the same in substance, essence, and nature *[that which defines God as God]*, but **they are different in office and person.**

THE HUMBLE FINITE ILLUSTRATION OF THE TRINITY:

The infinite GOD

cannot be fully described
by
a finite illustration

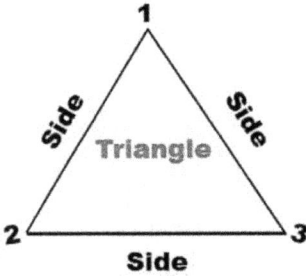

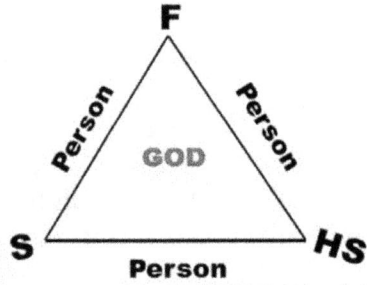

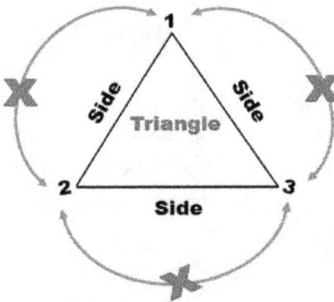

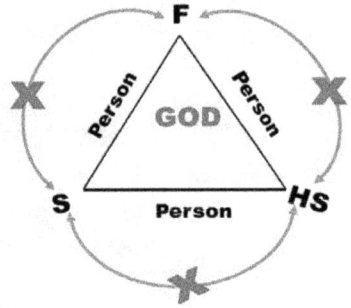

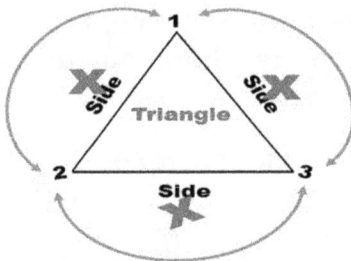

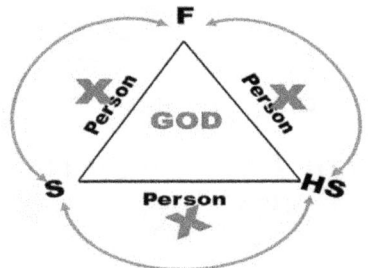

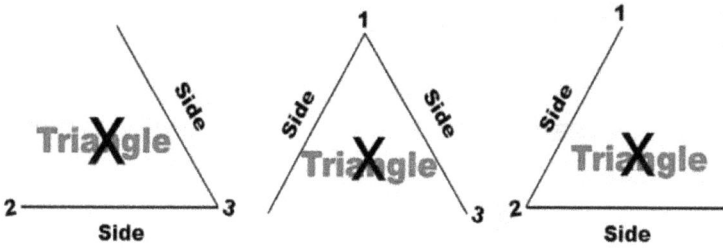

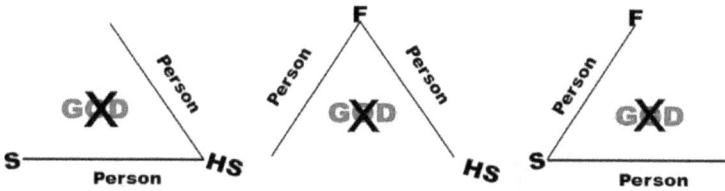

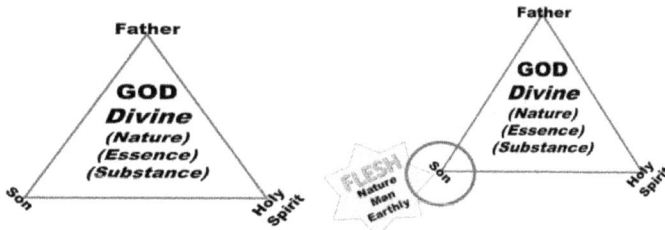

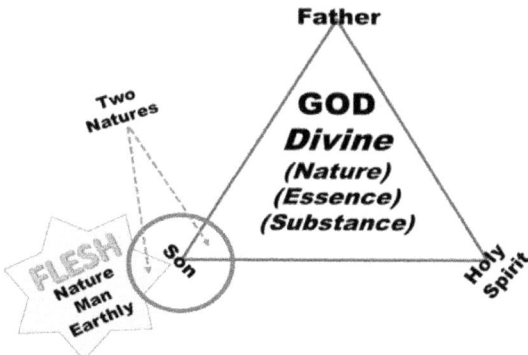

THE CHART FOR TRINITY THOUGHT:

	FATHER	SON	HOLY SPIRIT
Called God	Phil. 1:2	John 1:1, 14, Col. 2:9	Acts 5:3-4
Creator	Isaiah 64:8	John 1:3, Col. 1:15-17	Job 33:4, 26:13
Resurrects	1 Thess. 1:10	John 2:19, 10:17	Rom. 8:11
Indwells	2 Cor. 6:16	Col. 1:27	John 14:17
Everywhere	1 Kings 8:27	Matt. 28:20	Psalm 139:7-10
All-knowing	1 John 3:20	John 16:30, 21:17	1 Cor. 2:10-11
Sanctifies	1 Thess. 5:23	Heb. 2:11	1 Pet. 1:2
Life giver	Gen. 2:7, John 5:21	John 1:3, 5:21	2 Cor. 3:6, 8
Fellowship	1 John 1:3	1 Cor. 1:9	2 Cor. 13:14, Phil. 2:1
Eternal	Psalm 90:2	Micah 5:1-2	Rom. 8:11, Heb. 9:14
A Will	Luke 22:42	Luke 22:42	1 Cor. 12:11
Speaks	Matt. 3:17, Luke 9:25	Luke 5:20, 7:48	Acts 8:29, 11:12, 13:2
Love	John 3:16	Eph. 5:25	Rom. 15:30
Searches the heart	Jer. 17:10	Rev. 2:23	1 Cor. 2:10
We belong to	John 17:9	John 17:6	. . .
Savior	1 Tim. 1:1, 2:3, 4:10	2 Tim. 1:10, Titus 1:4, 3:6	. . .
We serve	Matt. 4:10	Col. 3:24	. . .
Believe in	John 14:1	John 14:1	. . .
Gives joy	. . .	John 15:11	John 14:7
Judges	John 8:50	John 5:22, 30	. . .

SCRIPTURE EVIDENCE FOR TRINITY DOCTRINE:

A.   **There is only One God (Deuteronomy 6:4).**
For There are three that bear witness record in heaven, the Father, the Word (Son (**John 1:1, 14**)), and the Holy Ghost: and these three are one. (**1 John 5:7**)

B.   **Three Persons Are Called God**
  1. **The Father is God**
    (Romans 1:7; Galatians 1:1; Matthew 6:9).
  2. **The Son is God**
    (Isaiah 9:6; Psalms 110:1; Hebrews 1:8; Zech. 12:10; John 8:58, Mark 2:5-7; John 5:23; Colossians 2:9; Titus 2:13)
  3. **The Holy Spirit is God**
    a. He has the names of God (God: **1 Corinthians 3:16; Lord: 2 Corinthians 3:17**)
    b. He has the attributes of God (**eternal: Hebrews 9:14; Omnipresence: Psalms 139:7; Omniscience: 1 Corinthian 2:11; Holiness: Ephesians 4:30**)
    c. He performs the acts of God (**creating: Genesis 1:2; Psalms 104:30; redeeming: Ephesians 4:30; doing miracles: Hebrews 2:4; giving supernatural gifts: 1 Corinthians 12:4-11**)
    d. He is associated with God in benedictions (**2 Corinthians 13:14**)
    e. He is associated with God in prayers (**Jude 1:20**).
    f. He has all the glory of God (**2 Corinthians 3:18**).
    g. He can be lied to (**Acts 5:3-4**)
    h. He can be grieved (**Ephesians 4:30**)
    i. He speaks (**Acts 13:2; 21:11**)
    j. He comforts (**John 14:26**)
    k. He bears witness (**Romans 8:16**)
    l. He hears (**John 16:13**)
    m. He makes intercession for us (**Romans 8:26**)

C. **All Three are Distinct Persons**
Person = one with **a mind**, **will**, and **feeling** (He can think, choose, and feel).
  1. **The Father is a Person**
    a. He has a mind (**Matthew 6:32**).
    b. He can choose (**Matthew 6:9-10**).
    c. He can feel (**Genesis 6:6**).
  2. **The Son is a Person**
    a. He has a mind (**John 2:25**).
    b. He can choose (**John 10:18**).
    c. He can feel (**John 11:35**).
  3. **The Holy Spirit is a Person**
    a. He has a mind (**John 14:26**).
    b. He can choose (**1 Corinthians 12:11**).
    c. He can feel (**Ephesians 4:30**).
D. **Hence, there are three distinct Persons in one God = The Trinity.**

TRINITY ACTING IN UNITY[98]

1. **In Creation:**
  a. **The Father**: God the Father spoke, (**Genesis 1:3**).
  b. **The Son** was the Word, (**John 1:1**); all things made through Him, (**John 1:3**).
  c. **The Holy Spirit**: God the Holy Spirit moved, (**Genesis 1:2. Job 26:12-13**).
2. **In the Incarnation:**
  a. **Father** gave His only Son, (**John 3:16**).
  b. **Son** born into the world, (**Luke 2:11**).
  c. **Holy Spirit** caused conception, (**Luke 1:35**).
3. **In Redemption:**
  a. **The Father** accepted the sacrifice of Calvary, (**Hebrews 9:14**).
  b. **The Son** offered Himself as the sacrifice, (**Hebrews 9:14**).
  c. **The Holy Spirit:** Jesus offered Himself through the Holy Spirit, (**Hebrews 9:14**).
4. **In Salvation:**
  a. **The Father** receives the prodigal, (**Luke 15:22**).

---

[98] Ultimate Cross Reference Treasury by Jerome Smith (2016): E-Sword Electronic Software

    b. **The Son** seeks the lost sheep, (**Luke 15:4; Luke 19:10**).

    c. **The Holy Spirit** seals the new convert, (**Ephesians 1:13**).

5. **In Communion:**

    a. **The Father** invites us to come to Him for fellowship, (**Ephesians 2:18**).

    b. **The Son** is the reconciliation, (**2 Corinthians 5:19**).

    c. **The Holy Spirit** effects union and communion, (**Ephesians 2:18**).

6. **In Prayer:**

    a. **The Father** receives our requests, (**John 16:23**).

    b. **The Son** is the One in whose Name we pray, (**John 16:23**).

    c. **The Holy Spirit** directs us in our requests, (**Romans 8:26**).

7. **In Glory:**

    a. **The Father** ultimately receives the millennial kingdom, (**1Corinthains 15:24**).

    b. **The Son** changes our body to be like His, (**Philippians 3:21**).

    c. **The Holy Spirit** gives the invitation, (**Revelation 22:17**).

8. **In Regeneration:**

    a. **The Father** records the new name in glory, (**Luke 10:20**).

    b. **The Son** cleanses sin in His blood, (**Ephesians 1:7**).

    c. **The Holy Spirit** performs the miracle of the new birth, (**John 3:3-8**).

9. **In the Resurrection of Christ:**

    a. **The Father**: God raised up Jesus, (**Acts 2:32**).

    b. **The Son**: Jesus said He raised **Himself from the dead**, (**John 2:19; John 10:18**).

    c. **The Holy Spirit** raised Jesus from the dead, (**Romans 8:11; 1 Peter 3:18**).

PLURALITY SCRIPTURES:

1. **Isaiah 44:6 (the Lord the King of Israel** and **his Redeemer** the Lord of hosts; I am the first and I am the last, and **besides me there is no God**).
2. **Isaiah 6:8** Also I heard the **voice of the Lord**, saying, Whom shall I send, and **who will go for us**? Then said I, Here am I; send me.
3. **Psalm 45:6 Thy throne, O God**, is for ever and ever: the sceptre of thy kingdom is a right sceptre. **Psalm 45:7** Thou lovest righteousness, and hatest wickedness: **therefore God, thy God**, hath anointed thee with the oil of gladness **above thy fellows**.
4. **Matthew 28:19** Go ye therefore, and teach all nations, baptizing them **in the name of the Father, and of the Son, and of the Holy Ghost**:
5. **Matthew 3:16** And **Jesus,** when he was baptized, went up straightway out of the water: and, lo, the heavens were opened unto him, and he saw **the Spirit of God descending like a dove**, and lighting upon him: 17And lo **a voice from heaven, saying, This is my beloved Son**, in whom I am well pleased.
6. **2 Corinthians 13:14** The grace of **the Lord Jesus Christ,** and **the love of God**, and **the communion of the Holy Ghos**t, be with you all. Amen.
7. **Genesis 1:26** And God said, **Let us** make man in our image, after **our likeness**: and let them have dominion over the fish of the sea, and over the fowl of the air, and over the cattle, and over all the earth, and over every creeping thing that creepeth upon the earth.
8. **Genesis 3:22** And the LORD God said, Behold, the man is become as **one of us**, to know good and evil: and now, lest he put forth his hand, and take also of the tree of life, and eat, and live for ever:
9. **Genesis 11:7** Go to, **let us** go down, and there confound their language, that they may not understand one another's speech. 8So the LORD scattered them abroad from thence upon the face of all the earth: and they left off to build the city.
10. **John 14:23** Jesus answered and said unto him, If a man love me, he will keep my words: and my

Father will love him, and **we will come** unto him, and make **our abode with him.**

11. **1 Corinthians 12:** 4 Now there are diversities of gifts, but the same Spirit. [5]And there are differences of administrations, but the same Lord.[6]And there are diversities of operations, **but it is the same God which worketh all in all**.

12. **Isaiah 42:8** I am the LORD: that is my name: and **my glory will I not give to another**, neither my praise to graven images.

13. **Isaiah 48:16** Come ye near unto me, hear ye this; I have not spoken in secret from the beginning; from the time that it was, **there am I**: and now **the Lord GOD**, and **his Spirit**, hath sent me.

14. **John 15:26** But when **the Comforter** is come, whom **I will** send unto you from **the Father**, even the Spirit of truth, which proceedeth from the Father, he shall testify of me:

15. **John 14:16** And **I will** pray **the Father**, and he shall give you **another Comforter**, that he may abide with you for ever;

THE EARLY CHURCH FATHERS:

- **Theophilus of Antioch** was the first person to use the Trinity that we have a record of it.

- **Irenaeus** sat out to write a list of every cult of his time. "Irenaeus Against Heresies"

- **Clements** also wrote using the word Trinity and a hymn about Christ praising him as God.

- **Tertullian** wrote about the Trinity. He came against Sabellians. He argued in favor of the Biblical doctrine of the Trinity. Called himself a Catholic, not Roman Catholic, but universal.

Theologians generally break down the attributes of God into two main categories:

- **Incommunicable attributes** – *The characteristics that God does not share with finite humanity but reserves for Himself alone.* This is where we truly realize that *God goes beyond what we can comprehend or even reveal.* But although we can never know God exhaustively we can know Him sufficiently. These attributes speak to God's divine nature that He has revealed about Himself and He wants us to know. These are also referred to as His non-moral attributes.

- **Communicable attributes** – *Those attributes that we can more directly identify.* Attributes that have been revealed in Scripture that *we can comprehend and reveal.* These usually speak to God's person and how He relates to creation. These are also referred to as His moral attributes.

CHAPTER EIGHT

THE CULTS AND JESUS

The term '**cult of Christianity**' is used of any group, church or organization whose central teachings and/or practices are claimed to be Biblical or representative of Biblical Christianity, but which are in fact unbiblical and not Christian in nature.

"The term '**cult of Christianity**' is more accurate than alternatives like '*Christian cult*,' or '*Bible-based cult*' - both of which essentially are oxymorons. After all, 'Christian cult' sounds as odd as 'Christian burglar.'

'**Bible-based cults**' often base their doctrines and practices on
- additional books and/or
- are known for their incorrect interpretation and
- application of the Bible.

That said, the latter two terms are frequently used in references to such groups." *[paraphrased]*[99]

More precisely, the definition of a "cult of Christianity" as defined by orthodox Christianity:

"a religious group that claims to be Christian, but the group denies one or more of the fundamentals of Biblical truth."

- A cult of Christianity is any group that teaches doctrines that, if believed, *will cause a person to remain unsaved*.

- A cult of Christianity claims to be part of orthodox religion, **yet it denies the essential truth(s) of orthodox religion**.

---

[99] http://www.apologeticsindex.org/2765-cult-of-christianity (April 7, 2017)

- Therefore, a Christian cult will deny one or more of the fundamental truths of Christianity while still claiming to be Christian.

THE JEHOVAH WITNESSES:

"Jesus lived in heaven as a spirit person before he was born on earth. (John 8:23) **He was God's first creation**, and **he helped in the creation of all other things. He is the only one created directly by Jehova**h and is thus called God's 'only-begotten' Son. Jesus served as God's Spokesman, so he is also called 'the Word.'" [100]

On the subject of the pre-incarnated Christ, they say that Jesus was Michael the Archangel. "Michael referred to by some religions as "Saint Michael," is evidently a name given to Jesus before and after his life on earth"[101]

The New World Translation: John 1:1 *"In the beginning was the Word, and the Word was with God, and the Word was **a god**."*[102]

Some Christians have been troubled by misinformed Jehovah's Witnesses who appear at their doors and argue that the Word (namely, the one who became flesh) was not actually God but was some lesser reality or a lower deity than God. Those misguided interpreters have sought to argue their case from the fact that the Greek word for God *(theos)* here does not have an article. Possessing a little Greek knowledge can sometimes lead to incorrect deductions and to very inappropriate theological conclusions. Simply because the Greek term "Word" *(logos)* here has an article and the Greek term for "God" *(theos)* lacks the article does not mean that the term "God" should be rendered as "**a god**.[103]

---

[100] https://www.jw.org/en/publications/magazines/wp20110301/who-is-jesus-christ/#?insight[search_id]=c038cbad-131a-4d07-850c-924aa2824cbf&insight[search_result_index]=2 (April 5, 2017)

[101] https://www.jw.org/en/bible-teachings/questions/archangel-michael/#?insight[search_id]=0af0c51e-21bd-47eb-abf3-c164c418aa94&insight[search_result_index]=1 (April 5, 2017)

[102] https://www.jw.org/en/publications/bible/nwt/books/john/1/ (April 5, 2017)

[103] Borchert, G. L. (1996). *John 1–11* (Vol. 25A, p. 103). Nashville: Broadman & Holman Publishers.

The New World Translation: Colossians 1: 15 *"He is the image of the invisible God, the firstborn of all creation; 16 because by means of **him all other things** were created in the heavens and on the earth, the things visible and the things invisible, whether they are thrones or lordships or governments or authorities. **All other things** have been created through him and for him. 17 Also, he is before all other things, and by means of him **all other things** were made to exist,"[104]*

*God created Jesus before creating Adam. In fact, God created Jesus and then used him to make everything else, **including the angels**. That is why the Bible **calls Jesus 'the firstborn of all creation' by God.***
*"THE **spirit creature** called Michael is not mentioned often in the Bible.*

*The Lord himself will descend from heaven with a commanding call, with an archangel's voice. Thus, the voice of Jesus is described as being that of an archangel. **This scripture, therefore suggests that Jesus himself is the archangel, Michael**.*

*Since God's Word nowhere indicates that there are two armies of faithful angels in heaven—**one headed by Michael** and **one headed by Jesus—it is logical to conclude that Michael is none other than Jesus Christ in his heavenly role**."[105]*

THE MORMONS:

Mormons also can't get out of John chapter one verse one.

---

[104] https://www.jw.org/en/publications/bible/nwt/books/colossians/1/ (April 5, 2017)
[105] https://www.jw.org/en/publications/books/bible-teach/who-is-michael-the-archangel-jesus/#?insight[search_id]=0b43a8cd-56fe-4228-a89c-3cd30197798c&insight[search_result_index]=2 (April 5, 2017)

> **John 1:1** *"In the beginning was the Word, and the Word was with God, and the Word was God."*

According to Mormon theology, God the Father is called **Elohim** and the Son (Jesus a separate god) is called **Jehovah**. The Mormons erroneously teach that God the Father was once a man, but "progressed" to godhood. He has a physical body, as does his wife (Heavenly Mother). In his pre-existence, Jesus was created in heaven as a spirit son through a relationship between Elohim (God the Father) and his heavenly wife. Jesus was the firstborn and Lucifer was the second born. They are spirit brothers. Mormons teach that the earthly body of Jesus was created by Elohim having a sexual relationship with Mary. Mormon theology is false and contrary to what the Apostle John writes. It is not "God breathed." According to Mormon theology, all of us were gods, including Lucifer.[106] Mormon theology completely butchers John chapter one.

The Mormons exist today because of what a 14-year boy, Joseph Smith, said. And today contrary to the Bible, many parents (some professed Christians) are giving into and are persuaded by what their 12-year-old children (and some younger) are saying about their gender confusion.

WORD FAITH MOVEMENT:

Some in the Word Faith Movement want to say Jesus is the Spoken Word. Jesus was literally produced by Speaking. They say, God just kept on speaking and speaking until Jesus came forth, which is a violation of John chapter one, which says, "In the beginning was the Word." According to their theology, everything is or has to be spoken. The Word Faith Movement does share New

---

[106] https://www.lds.org/scriptures/bofm?lang=eng (May 1, 2017)

Age aspects where in New Age all persons are gods. They teach that we are all little gods.

CHRISTIAN SCIENCE:

Science and Health with Keys to the Scripture. Christian Science beliefs about Jesus from Christian Science JSH-Online[107]

1. Christ is the spiritual idea of sonship *S&H* 331:30-31.
2. Jesus was not the Christ, *S&H* 333:3-15; 334:3.
3. "Jesus Christ is not God, as Jesus himself declared . . . " *S&H* 361:12-13.
4. Jesus did not reflect the fullness of God, *S&H* 336:20-21.
5. Jesus did not die, *S&H* 45:32-46:3.
6. The sacrifice of Jesus was not sufficient to cleanse from sin, *S&H* 25:6.

Christian Science believes that Jesus was not the Christ, but a man who exhibited the Christ idea. They believe that God can never become flesh, therefore Jesus was not God. He did not and could not suffer for sins. He did not die on the cross, nor was he resurrected physically. Jesus will not literally come back.[108]

SEVENTH-DAY ADVENTISM:

According to Adventists, God the Father exalted Jesus to be his Son, thus provoking Lucifer's jealousy and a war in heaven. Jesus is our example to prove we can live sinlessly. His sacrifice on the cross *did not complete the atonement*; since 1844 he has been applying his blood in heaven in an ongoing "Investigative Judgment" after which he will return.[109] Also identified as Michael the

---

[107] https://jsh.christianscience.com/ (April 26, 2017)
[108] Publishing, Rose. Christianity, Cults & Religions (Kindle Locations 223-226). Rose Publishing, Inc.. Kindle Edition.
[109] http://www.adventist.org/en/beliefs/restoration/christs-ministry-in-the-heavenly-sanctuary/ (April 26, 2017)

Archangel; most Adventist founders denied Jesus' deity."[110] Ultimately Satan will bear all of our sins, and when a person dies he does not exist anymore, that hell is not eternal.[111],[112]

ONENESS PENTECOSTAL:

Oneness Pentecostal theology affirms that there exists only one God in all the universe. Orthodox Christianity holds and affirms this monotheist view as well. Orthodox Christianity believes there is only one God who co-exists as three distinct eternal persons: The Father, The Son, and The Holy Ghost who are the same in essence, nature, and substance, but different only in person and in office. (*see chapter on the Trinity*).

However, Oneness Pentecostal theology denies the Biblical view of the Trinity and according to their doctrine, God is **a single person who was manifested:**[113],[114]

- **as the Father** in creation; **God revealed himself as Father** in the Old Testament.
- **as the Father** of the Son, in the **Son** for our redemption; **God revealed himself as the Son** in Jesus during Christ's ministry on earth.
- **as the Holy Spirit** in our regeneration. **God revealed himself now as the Holy Spirit after Christ's ascension.**

Oneness Pentecostalists *insist that Christians should be re-baptized 'in the name of Jesus only.'*[115] Oneness Pentecostalism defines salvation as repentance:

- baptism (**in Jesus' name**) and
- *receipt of a holy spirit,*

---

[110] Publishing, Rose. Christianity, Cults & Religions (Kindle Locations 167-171). Rose Publishing, Inc.. Kindle Edition.

[111] https://carm.org/seventh-day-adventism (April 26, 2017)

[112] https://news.adventist.org/en/all-news/news/go/1998-10-12/press-reports-quote-adventist-view-of-hell/ (April 26, 2017)

[113] http://www.upci.org/about/our-beliefs (April 7, 2017)

[114] https://carm.org/oneness-pentecostal-theology#footnote1_yylcf6e (April 7, 2017)

[115] http://www.apologeticsindex.org/2773-oneness-pentecostalism (April 7, 2017)

- with ***the evidence of speaking in other tongues***.[116]

Advocating a non-traditional view of God, Oneness Pentecostals find in modalistic Monarchianism of the fourth century a historical predecessor that affirmed the two central aspects of their own convictions:[117]

1. There is **one indivisible God** with no distinction of persons in God's eternal essence, and
2. Jesus Christ is the manifestation, human personification, or incarnation of the one God.[118]

Oneness Pentecostalism has a problem with what is stated and affirmed in John chapter one. As do all cults of Christianity, they must misinterpret the text for it to agree with their false theology. When we look at John 1 verse 1,

> *"In the beginning was the Word, and the Word was with God, and the Word was God."* (**John 1:1**)

Oneness Pentecostals must do something with this.

> if **the Word is Jesus** (and that is who it is)
>
> and ***the Word (Jesus)*** was **with** *God (the Father)*

Oneness Pentecostals know the same as us that this text is referring to at least two members (persons) of the Godhead. They are aware that all it takes is one more member, the Holy Spirit, and it would support the view of the Trinity. For Oneness Pentecostals that is a No ~ No!

But the question for them became what should they do with this text? They had to change (re-interpret) this verse to follow their theology. Looking at the text, they did some

---

[116] https://en.wikipedia.org/wiki/Oneness_Pentecostalism (April 7, 2017)
[117] https://en.wikipedia.org/wiki/Oneness_Pentecostalism (April 7, 2017)
[118] http://www.upci.org/about/about-oneness-pentecostalism (April 7, 2017)

lexical word analysis: *"In the* beginning was the Word, and the Word was with God and the Word was God."

They say **the Word** doesn't refer to Jesus. But **the Word** means *thought.* And they are right, the word does mean thought because Logos has more than just one meaning (thought, discourse, spoken).

But what the Oneness Pentecostal hopes that the Christian audience doesn't know is it that in the Greek mind (thought) the word Logos came to mean God. Therefore, God is a person and the person of God.

The Oneness Pentecostal wants to limit the usage of "the Word" to where it says, *"In the* beginning was the Word" and in Oneness theology, the Word becomes a thought in the Father's mind. If it is just a thought in the Father's mind then it is not a person. *"In the* beginning was the Word and the Word was with God" and it was with God in that it was in God's thinking (in God's mind). Notice it is not a person with him because if it were a person with him it would be too close to the Trinity. And according to Oneness theology, when the text says, "**the Word** was made flesh," that was just God coming down in the flesh. In other words, Jesus is the Father because he just came down in the word. So Jesus is God the Father, and this is where *oneness* comes from; Jesus is the Word, The Holy Spirit, and The Father.

Oneness understands that a word has a range of different meanings, just like any word does. But they want to choose just one aspect of the meanings, and one that complements their theology. They want to say that all Logos means is thought. Example, on a program called "Ask The Pastors," The Bishop Eric Clark said "The Word was the Thought, Plan, and Purpose of God," and "The Word was the Thought, Plan, and Purpose of God" was manifested in the flesh as the person of Christ. He also extends this to "we too are The Thought, Plan, and Purpose of God" that has become flesh.[119]

The Apostle John is appealing to the Greeks and knew that when the Greeks used Logos it connotes God. He uses a word that resonated with Greeks. However, regardless of whether you know the Greek meaning or not, the text makes it clear as to what John is writing about in context.

> **John 1:1** *"In the beginning was the Word, and the Word was with God,"*

But that is not all it says, it also says

"and the Word was God."

If the Word is God, it can't just be a thought in God's mind. If so, the thought is not God, but rather a thought in God's mind. But the next part of that verse is what traps Oneness: *"and the Word was God."* So, if the word is God it can't just be a thought in the mind of God. It must be equal. If you followed Oneness logic, it would make God just a thought. But Oneness theology doesn't press its faulty logic out to its conclusion, knowing it would suggest:

> *In the beginning was the Thought, and the Thought was in God's mind, and* **the Thought was God**.

Oneness Pentecostals admit that God is a single person. But the text establishes that not only is God a person, but the Word is a person as well.

For us, Scripture verifies Scripture. Oneness Pentecostals can't verify their claim because Scripture does not support it. They will try, however, to use

---

Scripture to show that Jesus is the Father to support their Oneness view. For example:

> **Isaiah 9:6** "*For unto us a child is born, unto us a son is given: and the government shall be upon his shoulder: and his name shall be called Wonderful, Counsellor, The mighty God, **The everlasting Father**, The Prince of Peace.*"

Oneness Pentecostals jump at this, saying "See he is called the Father. So, therefore, Jesus is the Father."

However, the Jews interpreted this to mean the Father of Creation. That is what *everlasting* connotes that the Father has eternality. The expression is rendered "the Father of Eternity" by Young in his *Literal Translation* and some other translations (Darby). The verse is not properly defining Jesus as the Father, but it is saying that He is the one responsible for creation as a member of the Godhead.

Every time the Bible uses the term *father* it is not using or saying it as a proper title. It could be used as in the creator or originator of something. For example, the "*father* of music" is not saying he is a father, but he is the one who created music. We see an example of this in Genesis where we begin to see how *father* is used other than a noun or in the sense of a man with children.

> "*And Adah bare Jabal: **he was the father of such as dwell in tents**, and of such as have cattle. 21 And his brother's name was Jubal: **he was the father of all such as handle the harp and organ**.*" (**Genesis 4:20**)

Does this mean that all the children he fathered were playing harps and organs? No. It means that he was the creator of these instruments.

Another verse Oneness advocates have trouble with which is difficult for them to get around:

> "*I, even I, have spoken; yea, I have called him: I have brought him, and he shall make his way prosperous.* ^{16} *Come ye near unto me, hear ye this; I have not spoken in secret from the beginning; from the time that it was, there **am I**: and now **the Lord God**, and **his Spirit**, hath sent me.*" (**Isaiah 48:15**)

Notice verse 21, We see:

1) God the great I am = "there am I"
2) And now the Lord God
3) And his Spirit

This is found all through the Bible, so Oneness adherents have to play some kind of hopscotch with all those Scriptures.

The Scripture shows Jesus praying to the Father. Clearly, the Apostle John writes of communication and relationship between the two (Father and Son), contrary to the claim of Oneness Pentecostal theology that God is **a single person who was manifested in three different modes.**

It is illogical to believe that Jesus on earth would be praying to himself in the mode of the Father in Heaven, and then as the Father in Heaven answer himself back on earth in the mode of Jesus.

- "*And Jesus lifted up his eyes, and said, **Father, I thank thee that thou hast heard me.*** ^{42} *And I knew that thou hearest me always: but because of the people which stand by I said it, that they may believe that thou hast sent me.*" (**John 11:41**)

- *"**Father, glorify thy name**. Then came there **a voice from heaven, saying, I have both glorified it**, and will glorify it again."* (**John 12:28**)

- *"And **I will pray the Father**, and **he** shall give you **another Comforter**, that he may abide with you for ever;"* (**John 14:16**)

Notice the words and context of John 14 verse 23. It just devastates Oneness Pentecostal theology. Here we have *Jesus* and the *Father* in the context of "**we**" and "**our**" showing at least two members (persons) of the Godhead coming and making their abode. But we are also told of the Holy Spirit coming in verse 14:26 and 15: 26. This is a demonstration of the Trinity coming and making their abode in context of the Scriptures:

- *"**Jesus** answered and said unto him, If a man love me, he will keep my words: and **my Father** will love him, and **we will come** unto him, and make **our abode** with him."* (**John 14:23**)
- *"But the Comforter, which is **the Holy Ghost**, whom **the Father** will send in **my name**, he shall teach you all things, and bring all things to your remembrance, whatsoever I have said unto you."* (**John 14:26**)
- *"As **the Father** hath loved **me**, so have I loved you: continue ye in my love."* (**John 15:9**)
- *"But when **the Comforter** is come, whom **I** will send unto you from **the Father**, even the **Spirit of truth**, which proceedeth from the **Father**, he shall testify of **me**:"* (**John 15:26**)
- *"These words spake Jesus, and lifted up his eyes to heaven, and **said, Father, the hour is come; glorify thy Son, that thy Son also may glorify thee:**"* (**John 17:1**)
- *"And now, **O Father**, glorify thou **me** with thine own self with the glory which **I had with thee** before the world was."* (**John 17:5**)

And what Luke tells us demonstrates that the **Modalism** view of Oneness Pentecostal theology does not work here:

"And when **Jesus** had cried with a loud voice, **he said, Father, into thy hands I commend my spirit:** and having said thus, he gave up the ghost."(**Luke 23:46**)

CHAPTER NINE

AND THEN THERE IS HELL

The Gospel of John is a very tough book on the issue of salvation.

> *"For God sent not his Son into the world to condemn the world; but that the world through him might be saved. 18 He that believeth on him is not condemned: but **he that believeth not is condemned already**, because he hath not believed in the name of the only begotten Son of God. 19 And this is the condemnation, that light is come into the world, and men loved darkness rather than light, because their deeds were evil."* (John 3:17-19)

John makes it clear that anyone who does not accept Jesus Christ is already condemned. If people die in a state of unbelief never accepting Jesus Christ as their Lord and personal Savior, they die in their sins.

> *"I said therefore unto you, that ye shall die in your sins: for **if ye believe not that I am he, ye shall die in your sins**."* (John 8:24)

Sadly, for them physical death is not the end and they don't go to heaven, but rather end up in hell.

Notice what Jesus tells us,

> *"Marvel not at this: for the hour is coming, in the which **all that are in the graves shall hear his voice**, 29 And shall come forth;*

> - *they that have done good, unto the resurrection of life; and*

- ***they that have done evil, unto the resurrection of damnation.***" **(John 5:28-29)**

The resurrection of damnation means the person who died in their sins will rise from the dead in a damnation body and in that body, they will be cast into hell. Jesus provides more details:

"*And if thy hand offend thee, cut it off: it is better for thee to enter into life maimed, than having two hands*
- ***to go into hell, into the fire that never shall be quenched:*** *^{44}* ***Where their worm dieth not, and the fire is not quenched.*** *^{45} And if thy foot offend thee, cut it off: it is better for thee to enter halt into life, than having two feet*
- ***to be cast into hell, into the fire that never shall be quenched:*** *^{46}* ***Where their worm dieth not, and the fire is not quenched.*** *^{47} And if thine eye offend thee, pluck it out: it is better for thee to enter into the kingdom of God with one eye, than having two eyes*
- ***to be cast into hell fire:*** *^{48}* ***Where their worm dieth not, and the fire is not quenched.***" **(Mark 9:43-48)**

"*And shall cast them into a furnace of fire:* ***there shall be wailing and gnashing of teeth.***" **(Matthew 13:42)**

"*And* ***the smoke of their torment ascendeth up for ever and ever:*** *and* ***they have no rest day nor night,*** *who worship the beast and his image, and whosoever receiveth the mark of his name.*" **(Revelation 14:11)**

The Scripture is clear that hell is where the person goes who does not accept Jesus Christ as their personal Savior. It is very important to know about hell. What it basically means is that one is separated from God throughout all eternity.

Now you might say, "Oh you just trying to make me afraid by frightening me." You are correct. **YES, I AM!**

In fact, the Bible recommends the fear tactic:

> *"Keep yourselves in the love of God, looking for the mercy of our Lord Jesus Christ unto eternal life.* [22] *And of some have compassion, making a difference:* [23]
>
> - ***And others save with fear,***
> - ***pulling them out of the fire;***
> - ***hating even the garment spotted by the flesh.***
>
> [24] *Now unto him that is able to keep you from falling, and to present you faultless before the presence of his glory with exceeding joy,"* (**Jude 21-24**)

Anybody with any sense should be afraid. Someone telling you that if you don't turn around, you are going to fall off the cliff, and you refuse to take heed? Healthy fear is good for you. Only people running around afraid of something that is not going to occur need psychiatric care. But in this case, hell is real and if you don't want to go there make sure that you are right with God. Simply, while the blood is running warm in your veins:

- *"That if thou shalt confess **with thy mouth the Lord Jesus,** and **shalt believe in thine heart that God hath raised him from the dead,** thou shalt be saved."* (**Romans 10:9**)

- *"Then Peter said unto them, **Repent,** and **be baptized every one of you in the name of Jesus Christ for the remission of sins,** and ye shall receive the gift of the Holy Ghost."* (**Acts 2:38**)

Yes, there are those who will say a loving God would not send anyone to hell to be tormented forever and ever for all eternity.

They are right! You send yourself when you choose to reject him. At the end of the day, what God is simply saying to you is, "Have it your way." You condemn yourself. It is not like God is going to send you to a place where you don't want to go. Nobody who goes to hell could survive a second in heaven, because they don't want to be there. In heaven, all it is going to be is worshipping God and His holiness. That is not the place for them. They go where they wanted to go which is into hell.

In fact, hell was not even made for man. God did not make hell as a place for a man to go.

> "*Then shall he say also unto them on the left hand, Depart from me, ye cursed, into everlasting fire, **prepared for the devil and his angels**:*" (**Matthew 25:41**)

So why would a person desire to go somewhere that was not made and designed for them? Hell was not designed for mankind. So it is simply a matter of choice.

> "*And this is the condemnation, that light is come into the world, **and men loved darkness rather than light**, because their deeds were evil. ²⁰ For **every one that doeth evil hateth the light**, neither cometh to the light, lest his deeds should be reproved.*" (**John 3:19-20**)

Everything in the universe belongs to God. God says at the end of the day I'm taking all that is mine and since you want no part of me, there you go.

Some groups such as the Jehovah Witnesses teach that there is no hell. They say that the dead (*non-Jehovah Witnesses*) are just annihilated. Ask them or any other recruiting group this question: "If you are wrong about hell, will you go to hell in my place?"

Physical Death: when you die, your body is buried and your soul continues either in hell (unbeliever) or with the Lord in heaven.

> "And it came to pass,

- *that the beggar died, **and was carried by the angels into Abraham's bosom**:*
- *the rich man also died, and was buried; 23 **And in hell he lift up his eyes, being in torments**, and seeth Abraham afar off, and Lazarus in his bosom.*" (**Luke 16:22-23**)

*"We are confident, I say, and willing rather **to be absent from the body, and to be present with the Lord**."(*2 Corinthians 5:8**)

And if people are living their life now in a state of unbelief while they are in the land of the living, even so, they are spiritually dead right now.

Spiritual Death: People who do not believe in Jesus Christ are dead right now spiritually. But the good news is that they can be recovered by accepting Jesus Christ as their personal savior, before dying physically. If they don't and they die in this state they go into the second death.

"And you hath he quickened, who **were dead in trespasses and sins**;" (**Ephesians 2:1**)
*"But she that liveth in pleasure **is dead while she liveth**.*" (**1 Timothy 5:6**)

The Bible informs us that:

Second Death: Physical death and Hades/sheol were cast into the second death. Here people are in an Irretrievable place: Hell, and they are separated from God for all eternity in a damnation body. This is everlasting death and punishment away from God.

*"Then shall he say also unto them on the left hand, Depart from me, **ye cursed, into everlasting fire**, prepared for the devil and his angels:*" (**Matthew 25:41**)
*"And **these shall go away into everlasting punishment**: but the righteous into life eternal.*" (**Matthew 25:46**)

> "And **death and hell** were cast into **the lake of fire.**
> This is **the second death."** (Revelation 20:14)

The cult called **Christian Science** teaches there is no death[120] and they don't believe in the Biblical hell. Death is not real. Heaven and hell are states of mind. The way to reach heaven is by attaining harmony (oneness with God).[121] They teach that "*Sin makes its own hell, and goodness its own heaven (S&H 196:18-19). The sinner makes his own hell by doing evil and the saint his own heaven by doing right (S&H 266:20-21).*[122] *The evil beliefs which originate in mortals are hell. Man is the idea of Spirit; he reflects the beatific presence, illuming the universe with light. Man is deathless, spiritual. He is above sin or frailty. He does not cross the barriers of time into the vast forever of Life, but he coexists with God and the universe. (SH 266-26).*" There is no devil, S&H 469:13-17. "Matter**, sin**, and sickness are not real, but only illusions," S&H 335:7-15; 447:27-28.[123]

Ellen G. White, founder of the cult Seventh-Day Adventism, "How repugnant to every emotion of love and mercy, and even to our sense of justice, is the doctrine that the wicked dead are tormented with fire and brimstone in an eternally burning hell; that for the sins of a brief earthly life they are to suffer torture as long as God shall live. Yet this doctrine has been widely taught and is still embodied in many of the creeds of Christendom."[124]

SALVATION

Far too often, when we're out witnessing, we meet people who say they are Christian, but when asked these simple questions:

---

[120] https://sentinel.christianscience.com/issues/1909/9/12-1/there-is-no-death (April 26, 2017)
[121] Publishing, Rose. Christianity, Cults & Religions (Kindle Locations 231-233). Rose Publishing, Inc.. Kindle Edition.
[122] https://sentinel.christianscience.com/issues/1909/9/12-1/there-is-no-death (April 26, 2017)
[123] https://carm.org/what-does-christian-science-teach (April 26, 2017)
[124] http://text.egwwritings.org/publication.php?pubtype=Book&bookCode=GC&lang=en&pagenumber=535 (April 26, 2017)

"God forbid, if you were to DIE tonight, where would you spend eternity?" Heaven or hell? *"If God were to ask you, Why, should I allow you to enter heaven, what would be your reply?"*

Too many answers range from:

A. *"**Well, I'm a Good Person**"*
   But the Bible says, *"They are all gone aside, they are all together become filthy: there is none that doeth good, no, not one."* (**Psalms 14:3**)
B. *"**Well, God Knows My Heart**"*
   But the Bible says, *"The heart is deceitful above all things, and desperately wicked: who can know it?"* (**Jeremiah 17:9**)
C. *"**I don't know**"*

Seldom do we hear, "The Bible says, ..."

It is incomprehensible for a person to say, *"**I'm a Christian"**** and have no clue what it means to say, *"**I'm saved**."*

Someone might ask:
1. **Saved from what?** Saved from what I justly deserved, eternal damnation (**John 5:29**), the Second Death (**Revelation 20:14**), I needed to be saved from myself and my sins.
   *"For the wages of **sin is death**; ..."* (**Romans 6:23**-a)
2. **Why do you need saving?** I realized that I could not save myself.
   - *"For sin, taking occasion by the commandment, **deceived me**, and by it **slew me**."* (**Romans 7:11**)
   - *"18 For **I know that in me** (that is, in my flesh,) dwelleth no good thing: for to will is present with me; but how to perform that which is good I find not. 19 For the good that I would I do not: **but**

the evil which I would not, that I do."
(**Romans 7:18-19**)

- "*8 For **by grace are ye saved** through faith; and that **not of yourselves**: it is the gift of God: 9 **Not of works**, lest any man should boast.*" (**Ephesians 2:8-9**)

3. **What must I do to be saved?** Accept and receive what God has done, repent, confess and believe.

- "*For God so loved the world, that **he gave his only begotten Son, that whosoever believeth in him should not perish**, but have everlasting life.*" (**John 3:16**)

- "*That if thou shalt **confess with thy mouth the Lord Jesus**, and shalt **believe in thine heart that God hath raised him from the dead**, thou shalt be saved. 10 For with the heart man believeth unto righteousness; and with the mouth confession is made unto salvation.*" (**Romans 10:9-10**)

- "*38 Then Peter said unto them, **Repent**, and be baptized every one of you in the name of Jesus Christ for the remission of sins, and ye shall receive the gift of the Holy Ghost.*" (**Acts 2:38**)

- "***Repent** ye therefore, and be **converted**, that **your sins may be blotted out**, when the times of refreshing shall come from the presence of the Lord;*" (**Acts 3:19**)

4. **What does it mean to say, "I'm a Saved Christian?"** We are followers of Him that has eternal life, Jesus Christ, who has reconciled and brought us back to God, the Father. For us, there is no other truth, way or life. He alone died and rose for us. We follow Christ.

- "*6 Jesus saith unto him, **I am the way, the truth, and the life**: no man cometh unto the Father, but by me.*" (**John 14:6**)

- "*6 For when we were yet without strength, in due time **Christ died for the ungodly**. 7 For scarcely for a righteous man will one die: yet*

> *peradventure for a good man some would even dare to die. 8 But God commendeth his love toward us, in that,* **while we were yet sinners, Christ died for us***. 9 Much more then,* **being now justified by his blood***, we shall be saved from wrath through him.*" (**Romans 5:6-9**)

The Christian understands the implication of saying, **"I'm saved."** I've passed from death to life.

> "... *but* **the gift of God is eternal life through Jesus Christ** *our Lord.*" (**Romans 6:23**-b)

The Christian should always be ready to give a Biblical answer when asked, "Why do you believe you're going to heaven?" *"Because God said it in Scripture, Jesus sealed it, and I believe the Word of God. Nothing more and nothing less."*

And Then There is Hell

CHAPTER TEN

CHRISTIANS ARE COMMAND TO JUDGE!

Often, the Scripture provides the adequate meaning of the usage of a word in the very context in which it was used within a verse or verses. Many words have multiple meanings. A language lexicon is good and can provide the various definitions of a given word, but it may or may not point to the precise meaning the author intended in a verse. Time, language barriers, etc. can have an impact on the usage or development of a given word. For example, the word "gay" used to refer to a person that was happy, lighthearted and carefree. Today, it is considered a derogatory term referring to a person who is homosexual, lesbian, or queer.

With the words Judge, Judgment, and Judgmental it becomes a matter of by whom or by what authority? Who executes the judgment? And who are the recipients of it? No matter what the answer is, nothing happens without God allowing it or unless it is according to His will.

People will say, *"you can't judge me--only the man (God) upstairs can judge me."* But they are both wrong and right with their assertion. If they break the law, they go before a judge (a person) and perhaps a jury of their peers (twelve people) in whose hands God has placed their earthly fate (and some cases the death penalty). Even so, should the person not repent, they face the ultimate Judge and Judgment (condemnation).

Now we could do a word play as to whether it is "judging or discerning" or "Judgment versus Discernment," but for the Biblical Christian, isn't it supposed to be Scripture interprets Scripture? It is never about what you or I say it means, but what did the Biblical author mean and in what context; understanding that all Scripture is God-Breathed.

COMPETENT TO JUDGE[125]:

Paul deemed individuals competent to judge the truthfulness and correctness of the teaching of the apostles:

> "*But though* **we**, *or an angel from heaven,* **preach any other gospel unto you than that which we have preached unto you**, *let him be accursed.*" (**Galatians 1:8**; see **Acts 17:11**)

Is not Paul saying judge us based on the evidence that you heard and now hear flowing from our lips? You be the judge of whether we have changed and now preach another gospel. Today, are pastors preaching a different gospel than what we read and comprehend in our Bibles? Shouldn't we be like the Bereans?

> "... *they received the word with all readiness of mind, and searched the scriptures daily, whether those things were so.*" (**Acts 17:11**)

JUDGE NOT ACCORDING TO APPEARANCE:

Jesus said:
> "**Judge not according to the appearance**, but judge righteous judgment." (**John 7:24; Deuteronomy 1:16**)

NO! Jesus did **NOT SAY DON'T** judge. The question that should be asked is what did Jesus mean? Knowledge of verses context:

The Law of **Moses** on circumcision (**Leviticus 12:3**) [which actually, originated with covenant and practiced (**Genesis 17:9-14**) by **the 'fathers,'** that is, by Abraham, Isaac, Jacob] commanded that a male child

---

should be circumcised eight days after birth. **Even if the eighth day fell on the Sabbath**, the Jews did not consider it wrong to **circumcise** the baby boy. They felt that it was a work of necessity and that the Lord allowed for such a work.

The Jews had sought to make the observance of the sabbath more rigorous than God had commanded. It was not wrong to eat on the sabbath, even if the food must be obtained by plucking corn from the ears. Nor was it wrong to do good on the sabbath day. To heal was a work of mercy, and the Lord of the sabbath is merciful (cf. also **John 5:1–18; Luke 13:10–17; 14:1–6).**[126]

"The Old Testament does not forbid cures on the sabbath day, but the rabbis, traditionally, labeled all healing as work which must always be avoided on the sabbath unless life was at risk. Jesus fearlessly exposed the callousness and absurd inconsistencies to which this attitude led. How, he asked, could it be right to circumcise a baby or lead an animal to water on the sabbath day (which tradition allowed), but wrong to heal a chronically handicapped woman and a crippled man—even if their lives were not in immediate danger **(Luke 13:10–17; John 7:21–24)**?[127]

Jesus had just charged the Jews of **not keeping the law of Moses by wanting to kill him** (Exodus 20:13) him (John 7:19).

The Jews had accused Jesus of breaking the sabbath by healing:
> "Jesus saith unto him, **Rise, take up thy bed, and walk.** 9 And immediately **the man was made whole**, and took up his bed, and

---

[126] Young, E. J., & Bruce, F. F. (1996). Sabbath. In D. R. W. Wood, I. H. Marshall, A. R. Millard, J. I. Packer, & D. J. Wiseman (Eds.), *New Bible dictionary* (3rd ed., p. 1032). Leicester, England; Downers Grove, IL: InterVarsity Press.
[127] Elwell, W. A., & Beitzel, B. J. (1988). Sabbath. In *Baker encyclopedia of the Bible* (Vol. 2, p. 1877). Grand Rapids, MI: Baker Book House.

walked: **and on the same day was the sabbath**. [10] The Jews therefore said unto him that was cured, It is the sabbath day: **it is not lawful** for thee to carry thy bed. [16] And **therefore did the Jews persecute Jesus, and sought to slay him, because he had done these things on the sabbath day**." **(John 5:8-10, 16)**

Jesus says that the Jews were performing circumcision (by Law) on a man, contrary to the law of the Sabbath **(Exodus 20:8-11)**

(On John 7:23) If they circumcised a child **on the Sabbath**, in order to obey **the law of Moses** regarding circumcision, why should they find fault with the Lord Jesus for making **a man completely well on the Sabbath**? If the law allowed for a work of necessity, would it not also allow for a work of mercy?[128]

(On John 7:19) "The Law of Moses was clear in its position against murder, yet that is precisely what rested in their hearts during this conversation. In spite of all their bragging, their villainous hearts betrayed their own breaking of the law." [129]

(on John 7:21–24. "But enough talk about Moses—circumcision came from Abraham. **It had to be observed on the eighth day after birth, so occasionally it would fall on the Sabbath**. Since this righteous act marked purification, why could not cleansing and healing be acceptable on the Sabbath? Godet paraphrases Jesus' point: 'It is precisely *for this*, that is to say, with the design of teaching you not to judge as you are doing—when you are scandalized ...

---

[128] MacDonald, W. (1995). *Believer's Bible Commentary: Old and New Testaments*. (A. Farstad, Ed.) (p. 1510). Nashville: Thomas Nelson.
[129] Gangel, K. O. (2000). *John* (Vol. 4, p. 145). Nashville, TN: Broadman & Holman Publishers.

at my Sabbath work—that Moses did not hesitate to impose the rite of circumcision upon you, while introducing into his **law this conflict with the law of the Sabbath**. Thereby, he has justified me in advance, by making all of you commit the transgression for which you are seeking to kill me' (Godet, p. 66)."[130]

The Lord Jesus had not broken the Law of Moses; it was they who were breaking it by their senseless hatred of Him.[131]

Do you show hatred and judge according to appearance, when others bring sound Biblical doctrine to you that conflicts with what your pastor teaches or what you choose to believe?

Isn't it strange that the very people who at a whim are ready to say, "*We are not supposed to judge,*" are often the very people doing just that, and doing it not according to righteousness?

BE NOT UNEQUALLY YOKE: DISCERNMENT:

"Paul's difficult instruction was that believers should **not be yoked together with unbelievers.** Paul probably alluded **to Deuteronomy 22:10, which prohibited the yoking together of oxen and donkeys**. Like many other Mosaic laws which may seem odd to us today, this prohibition taught Israel through symbolism that they were to remain pure by separating themselves from the surrounding Gentile nations. Paul used this law in much the same way here.

It is common for Christians to apply Paul's instruction here to marriages and close business associations between believers and unbelievers. Paul taught against marrying outside the faith, and wisdom should be exercised in all business relationships. Yet, in this

---

[130] Gangel, K. O. (2000). *John* (Vol. 4, pp. 145–146). Nashville, TN: Broadman & Holman Publishers.
[131] MacDonald, W. (1995). *Believer's Bible Commentary: Old and New Testaments.* (A. Farstad, Ed.) (p. 1510). Nashville: Thomas Nelson.

passage, Paul focused on all associations with unbelievers that led to infidelity to Christ, particularly by involvement with pagan rituals and idol worship. Paul wanted the Corinthian believers to separate themselves from these practices."[132]

"Be ye not unequally yoked together with unbelievers: for what fellowship hath **righteousness** with **unrighteousness**? and what communion hath **light** with **darkness**? [15] And what concord hath **Christ** with **Belial**? or what part hath **he that believeth** with **an infidel**?" **(2 Corinthians 6:14-15)**

WHY THE CHURCH IS INSTRUCTED TO JUDGE:

Sexual Immorality Defiles the Church. The truth is that God has given a charge to sinners saved by grace. There is none (from the least to the greatest--from the brother to the Bishop) who should be **allowed to practice sin** in the body of Christ and it goes unchallenged. When these things are known, and reported, and evidenced, the church (body of Christ) is accountable.

Paul presents a case so clear that one could scream until the cows come home, "**YOU CAN'T JUDGE ME!**" Paul says, "I've already pronounced judgment on the one who did such a thing" (1 Corinthians 5:3).

He instructs the church that the one who has done this sinful practice be removed from the church (1 Corinthians 5:2).
The problem today is that people can practice sin in one church, and another church receives them with open arms. No letter is required from the previous church. Just welcome to the hen house. People can bounce from one church to another with no accountability.

---

[132] Pratt, R. L., Jr. (2000). *I & II Corinthians* (Vol. 7, p. 375). Nashville, TN: Broadman & Holman Publishers.

Excommunication is thought of as unloving, as if we know better than Apostle Paul, who said,

"you are to deliver this man to Satan for the destruction of the flesh, so that his spirit may be saved in the day of the Lord." (1 Corinthians 5:5)

Apostle Paul reminds and asks the church:

"Do you not know that a little leaven leavens the whole lump?" (1 Corinthians 5:6)

Apostle Paul instructs the church:

"Cleanse out the old leaven that you may be a new lump, as you really are unleavened." (1 Corinthians 5:6)

Apostle Paul informs the church regarding permissible associations with specific instructions for those inside its walls ~ [so called] Christians ~ brothers and sisters of the faith:

*"I wrote to you in my letter not to associate with **sexually immoral people**"* (1 Corinthians 5:10)

*"But now I am writing to you **not to associate with anyone who bears the name of brother** if he is guilty of sexual immorality or greed, or is an idolater, reviler, drunkard, or swindler—**not even to eat with such a one**."* (vs 11)

Then contrary to what we hear so many Christians say, Apostle Paul says:

*"For what have I to do with judging outsiders? **Is it not those inside the church whom you are to judge?**"* (1 Corinthians 5:12)

*"....**Purge the evil person from among you**."*
(vs 13) (**1 Corinthians 5** (ESV)).

As to the people on the outside of the body of Christ, Paul says:

*"9 I wrote to you in my letter not to associate with sexually immoral people— 10 **not at all meaning the sexually immoral of this world, or the greedy and swindlers, or idolaters, since then you would need to go out of the world**.*

12 For What have I to do with judging outsiders? 13 God judges those outside...." (**1 Corinthians 5** (ESV))

A DAY FOR RIGHTEOUS JUDGING:

When one of you has a grievance against another, does he dare go to law before the unrighteous instead of the saints? 2 Or do you not know that the saints will judge the world? And if the world is to be judged by you, are you incompetent to try trivial cases? 3 Do you not know that we are to judge angels? How much more, then, matters pertaining to this life! 4 So if you have such cases, why do you lay them before those who have no standing in the church? 5 I say this to your shame. Can it be that there is no one among you wise enough to settle a dispute between the brothers, (**1 Corinthians 6:1-5 (ESV)**)

HYPOCRITICAL JUDGING:

"Judge not, that ye be not judged. 2 For with what judgment ye judge, ye shall be judged: and with what measure ye mete, it shall be measured to you again. 3 And why beholdest thou the mote that is in thy brother's eye, but considerest not the beam that is in thine own eye? 4 Or how wilt thou say to thy brother, Let me pull out the mote out of thine eye; and, behold, a beam is in thine own eye? 5 Thou hypocrite, first cast out the beam

out of thine own eye; and then shalt thou see clearly to cast out the mote out of thy brother's eye." (**Matthew 7:1-5 (KJV)**))

Christians Are Command to Judge!

CHAPTER ELEVEN

CHRISTIAN WARFARE

CHRISTIAN WARFARE
- **Ephesians 6:10-20 "stand against the wiles of the devil"**;
- **Corinthians 10:4** "the weapons of **our warfare** are not carnal";
- **James 4:7 "Resist the devil"**;
- **1 Peter 5:8-9** "Be sober, be vigilant; because **your adversary the devil**, as a roaring lion, walketh about, seeking whom he may devour: ⁹ **Whom resist stedfast in the faith"**

CHRISTIAN PREPARATION
- **2 Timothy 2:15** "Study"
- **1 Thessalonians 5:21** "hold fast that which is good";
- **John 14:6** "The way"
- **1 Corinthians 12:10** "discerning of spirits";
- **1 John 4:2-3** "Every spirit that confesseth that Jesus Christ is come"

CHRISTIAN WEAPONS/TOOLS
- **John 1:1** "The Word";
- **2 Timothy 3:16** "All Scripture";
- **John 15:3–7** "Without Jesus I can do nothing/ Abide in Him"
- **Philippians 4:13 "I can do all** things through Christ which strengtheneth me"

RULER OF THIS WORLD
- **Ephesians 2:2** "prince of the power of the air"; **2 Corinthians 4:4** - "the god of this world/age"
- **Ephesians 6:10-20** "the rulers of the darkness of this world/age"; **John 14:30** - "the prince of this world"
- **1 Corinthians 10:20** "fellowship with devils"; **Deuteronomy 32:17** - "They sacrificed unto devils"

- **1 John 4:4** "greater is he that is in you, than he that is in the world."

SATAN WANTS TO BE WORSHIPPED

- **1 Timothy 4:1** "doctrines of devils";
- **2 Corinthians 11:13-14** - "Satan himself is transformed into an angel of light"
- **Luke 4:5-7** "If thou therefore wilt worship me";
- **2 Timothy 3:5** "Having a form of godliness";
- **Ezekiel 28:1-36** – "Lucifer";
- **Isaiah 14:12-21** "I will be like the Most High"
- **2 Corinthians 11:4** "Preaching another Jesus, or if ye receive another spirit, or another gospel"

SATAN AND HIS ANGELS AND AGENTS' FALL

- **Luke 10:18** "beheld Satan as lightning fall from heaven";
- **Matthews 25:41** "everlasting fire, prepared for the devil and his angels"
- **Revelation 19:20** "Beast/False prophet: These both were cast alive into a lake of fire burning with brimstone."
- **Revelation 20:10** "the devil that deceived them was cast into the lake of fire and brimstone"
- **Revelation 20:2-3** "the dragon, that old serpent, which is the Devil, and Satan and bound him a thousand years / And cast him into the bottomless pit"
- **1 Peter 3:19** "the spirits in prison";
- **2 Peter 2:4** "God spared not the angels that sinned, but cast them down to hell, and delivered them into chains of darkness"

GOD LIMITS SATAN

- **Genesis 50:20** "ye thought evil against me; but God meant it unto good"
- **Job 1:12** "only upon himself put not forth thine hand";
- **Job 2:6** "he is in thine hand; but save his life"

- **Psalm 24:1** "The earth is the LORD's, and the fulness thereof; the world, and they that dwell therein."

SATAN & MIRACLES, SIGNS, AND WONDERS

- **Exodus 7:10–12** "Pharaoh called the wise men and **the sorcerers/the magicians**, they also did in like manner with their enchantments and cast down their rods, and they became serpents"
- **2 Thessalonians 2:9** "Even him, whose coming is after the working of Satan with all **power** and **signs** and **lying wonders**"
- **Deuteronomy 13:1-3, 5** "If there arise among you a **prophet**, or a **dreamer of dreams**, and giveth thee **a sign or a wonder**/Thou shalt not hearken"

GOD FORBIDS ALL FORMS OF OCCULT PRACTICES

- **Samuel 28:1-25; 1 Chronicles 10:13-14**; "Saul consulted a **medium** for guidance, instead of the Lord"
- **Leviticus 19:26** "neither shall ye use **enchantment**, nor **observe times**"; **Exodus 22:18** "Thou shalt not suffer a **witch** to live";
- **Leviticus 19:31** "Regard not them that have **familiar spirits**, neither seek after **wizards,** to be defiled by them"
- **Deuteronomy 18:9-12** "**pass through the fire**, or that **useth divination**, or **an observer of times**, or **an enchanter**, or a **witch**, or a **charmer**, or a **consulter with familiar spirits**, or a **wizard**, or a **necromancer**"
- **Isaiah 47:12-14** "Stand with thine **enchantments/** thy **sorceries**/Let now the **astrologers**, the **stargazers**, the monthly **prognosticators**, stand up, and save thee";
- **Galatians 5:20** "Idolatry, witchcraft"
- **Acts 13:6-12** "Paul withstands Barjesus/Elymas the **sorcerer/false prophet** seeking to turn away the deputy from the faith"

- **Acts 19:13-20** "[Seven sons of a Jewish high priest named Sceva] confessing and divulging their practices. / those who **practiced magic arts** brought their books together and burned them in the sight of all;"
- **Acts 16:16-20** "girl with **a spirit of divination** and brought her owners much gain by **soothsaying**"
- **2 Corinthians 2:11** "Lest Satan should get an advantage of us: for **we are not ignorant of his devices**"

SATAN'S INFLUENCES

- **Satan** Affects Lives (Job 1:6-9; 2:1–4)
  o **Satan** Can Cause Pain-Illness (Job 1:18-19; 2:7; Acts 10:38; 1 Cor 5:5)
- **Satan** Affects Finances (Job 1:14–17)
  o **Satan** Influences World Events (Dan 10:13)
- **Satan** Affects Personal Relationships (Job 1 & 2; John 7)
  o **Satan** Influences Political Events (Matt 2; Rev 12)

INTERPRETATION OF DREAMS BELONGS TO GOD

- **Genesis 40:7–8** "Joseph said unto them, Do not interpretations belong to God?"
- **Isaiah 8:19** "when they shall say unto you, Seek unto them that have **familiar spirits**, and unto **wizards that peep**, and that mutter: should not a people **seek unto their God?** for the living to the dead?"
- **Isaiah 45:11** "Thus saith the LORD, the Holy One of Israel, and his Maker, **Ask me of things to come** concerning my sons, and concerning the work of my hands command ye me"
- **Daniel 2:27-28** Daniel answered the king, "No **wise men**, **enchanters**, **magicians**, or **astrologers** can show to the king the mystery which the king has asked, / **but there is a God in heaven who reveals mysteries**";

- **Daniel 1:17-20** "he found them **ten times better than all the magicians and astrologers** that were in all his realm"

WE CAN NOT COMMUNICATE WITH DEAD PEOPLE

- **Luke 16:19–31** "between us and you **there is a great gulf fixed**: so that they which would pass from hence to you cannot; neither can they pass to us, that would come from thence." See Isaiah 63:16.
- **2 Corinthians 5:6-8** "whilst we are at home in the body, we are absent from the Lord / I say, and willing **rather to be absent from the body, and to be present with the Lord**"

TWO KINDS OF ANGELS
- **God's Angels – Spirit-beings**
  - Sent by God (Ex.23:30),
  - Accountable to God (Job 2:1),
  - Respond to God's will (Ps. 91:11),
  - God chooses which angel (Matt. 18:10),
  - Fulfill God's will (Luke 4:10),
  - Speak in the name of God (Luke 1:28),
  - Bring awe, respect, fear (Luke 1:11–13).
- **Fallen Angels – Demons – Spirit-beings**
  - Oppose God,
  - Requested by humans,
  - Respond to rituals (at their will),
  - We choose our favorite angel,
  - Fulfill our will (at first),
  - Speak like us (if they choose),
  - Appear friendly and natural to us.

  Satan/Lucifer is a created being:
  - **Ezekiel 28:15** "Thou wast perfect in thy ways from the day that thou **wast created**, till iniquity was found in thee."
  - **Psalm 148:1–5** "for he commanded, and **they were created**";
  - **Colossians 1:16** "For by him were all things created"

- **Demons are intelligent**, but not omniscient:
  - **Mark 1:24** "demons were aware of who Jesus was";
  - **Matthew 8:29** - "demons were aware ultimate destiny";
  - **1 Timothy 4:1** – "Paul refers to doctrines of demons"
- **Demons are localized**, but not omnipresent:
  - **Matthew 8:28–34** "sought Jesus not to send them out of the country"; Acts 16:16;
- **Demons are powerful**, but not omnipotent:
  - **Mark 5:3-4** "break chains/no one could bind the man";
  - **Mark 9:22** "cast boy into fire and water";
  - **Matthew 9:32** – "impaired speech of a man";
  - **Matthew 15:22** - "Kept girl in cruel vexation";
  - **John 10:21** "demons are limited in their powers, can't do what God can do"

CHAPTER TWELVE

CHARLES TEMPLETON

I asked Pastor Moss his thoughts on whether a person could step outside the boundaries of what God has revealed in his Word? How is it possible that a person can move from seeking, preaching, and teaching about God to suddenly not believing in God? I had in mind Charles Templeton.

Charles Templeton was converted to Christianity about 1936 and later became an evangelist in 1941.[133] He and Billy Graham were both rising lights in the Christian world and instrumental in founding Youth for Christ. He attended Princeton Theological Seminary, he hosted weekly television shows, but after struggling with doubt he declared himself an agnostic and publicly pronounced that he had lost his faith.

Well, said Pastor Moss, I read a book by Irwin H. Linton, *A Lawyer Examines the Bible*, where he said that of all the skeptics that he met not even a single one of them had ever read the evidence for the Christian faith. They had many questions, questions they had gotten from reading atheistic authors, but they had read nothing, not so much as one of the classic works defending the Bible and the Christian faith, scholarly works that present the evidence that proves the Christian faith to be true. Any person who would carefully read these classic works on Christian Evidences would be convicted by the evidence. He said that the big problem is that people don't look at both sides of the issues—they have never faced the best defenses ever written and answered them.

You rarely find an atheist who has read apologetics. They read books by other atheists. They have no clue as to the facts and logic of the other side.

---

[133] https://en.wikipedia.org/wiki/Charles_Templeton (12/01/2016)

So, in the case of Templeton, he was believing, but he was believing without the evidence. It is not that they went too far out. They never searched out both sides of the issue in a lawyer-like manner in the first place. Even Billy Graham, as good of an evangelist as he is, he isn't a strong apologist. Neither Templeton nor Graham studied evidence back in that day. Billy Graham may have studied some later. But basically, he just said I'm going to believe the Bible as the Word of God, and God blessed him for it. He just happened to be believing something, the Bible, that is backed up by the evidence. But Templeton, he didn't study any apologetics. He simply had questions about the Bible and couldn't get answers. He had problems with the evil in the world.

I defy anybody to read the evidence.

> http://www.godandscience.org/apologetics/evidence_and_christian_faith.html
> Sir William Mitchell Ramsay was a highly respected archaeologist (so much so that he was knighted) from Scotland. He set out to prove the historical inaccuracies of the book of Acts. Ramsay thought this book was the most ridiculous of all the New Testament. He spent fifteen years researching and digging, only to end up being convinced of the incredible accuracy of the book. He converted to Christianity, and called Luke (who wrote Acts) one of the greatest historians to ever live. He has written several books on the subject, which have yet to be refuted. His work caused an outcry from atheists because they had been eagerly awaiting his results in disproving the validity of the book.[134]

---

[134] http://askawiseman.com/skeptics/ (12/01/2016)

CHAPTER THIRTEEN

WOULD YOU LIKE TO ACCEPT CHRIST, TODAY?

Would you like to enter the Kingdom of God? It is simply a matter of being born again from above.

Do you confess with your mouth that you are a sinner; and believe that Jesus Christ died for your sins (**Romans 10:9-10**); and that He rose on the third day never to die again?

If you do, may I encourage you to pray a simple prayer of repentance?

Please understand that it is not this or any other prayer that saves you. It is only through trusting in Christ that can save you from your sins.

This prayer is simply a way to express to God your faith in Him and thank Him for providing for your salvation.

"God, I know that I have sinned against you and am deserving of punishment. But Jesus Christ took the punishment that I deserve so that through faith in Him I could be forgiven. I place my trust in You for salvation. Thank You for Your wonderful grace and forgiveness—the gift of eternal life! Amen!"

If you prayed that prayer, welcome to the Body of Christ! Now that you have given your life to Christ, in obedience to Him, you want to find a good Bible teaching church (**Hebrews 10:24-25**) and be baptized (**Acts 2:38; 8:35--37**). If you like, I can help you with that. You can write, email, or call me. My information is in the back of the book.

Here are a few verses about your salvation; what God has done to you:

*"And you hath **he quickened**, who were dead in trespasses and sins;"* (**Ephesians 2:1**)

"*Therefore if any man be in Christ, **he is a new creature**: old things are passed away; behold, all things are become new.*" (**2 Corinthians 5:17**)

"*We know that **we have passed from death unto life**, because we love the brethren. He that loveth not his brother abideth in death.*" (**1 John 3:14**)

"[29] *Take my yoke upon you, **and learn of me**; for I am meek and lowly in heart: and ye shall find rest unto your souls. [30] For my yoke is easy, and my burden is light.*" (**Matthew 11:29-30**)

Did you make your decision to accept Jesus Christ based on what you read in this book?

We would love to hear from you!

APPENDIX

GLOSSARY

AD, BC, BCE and CE:
AD is Anno Domini or Year of our Lord referring to the year of Christ's birth.
BC is Before Christ.
CE is a recent term. It refers to Common Era and is used in place of A.D. the dates are the same i.e., 2009 AD is 2009 CE.
BCE means Before Common Era. For example, 400 BC is 400 BCE.

Angelology comes from the Greek word, "angelos," which means angel and the Greek word, "logos," which means word or study. Therefore, angelology is the study of angels. The English word *angel* occurs more than 290 times in the Bible.
The Old Testament was written in Hebrew and Hebrew word for Angel is "malak." An Angel is a messenger of God. Biblically speaking, angels (sent ones who are not humans) are created beings, who are very powerful.[135]

Antilegomena: Literally, the books "spoken against," that is, the books of the new Testament canon whose inspiration has been disputed, usually meaning (NT) Hebrews, James, 2 Peter, 2 and 3 John, Jude, and Revelation. (OT) Esther, Proverbs, Song of Solomon, Ecclesiastes, and Ezekiel.

Apocryphal Books: Deuterocanonical books 14 Books in the O.T. not deemed as inspired scriptures by Protestants, but later accepted as scripture by the Roman Catholics - Council of Trent 1546AD. They were written in the inter-testimental period (silent years).

Apologetics may be simply defined as the defense of the Christian faith.

---

[135] https://carm.org/dictionary-angelology (May 21, 2017)

Apostasy is the falling away from the Christian faith. It is a revolt against the truth of God's Word by a believer. It can also describe a group or church organization that has "fallen away" from the truths of Christianity as revealed in the Bible.

Apotheosis: Man becoming a god.
(from Greek ἀποθέωσις from ἀποθεοῦν, *apotheoun* "to deify"; in Latin *deificatio* "making divine"; also called **divinization** and **deification**) is the glorification of a subject to divine level. The term has meanings in theology, where it refers to a belief, and in art, where it refers to a genre. In theology, *apotheosis* refers to the idea that an individual has been raised to godlike stature. In art, the term refers to the treatment of any subject (a figure, group, locale, motif, convention or melody) in a particularly grand or exalted manner.

Autoptic (au·top·tic) :
relating to or belonging to personal observation (A view of Its own) **[The Book of John]**

Atheism: Atheism denies the existence of God, either in the universe or beyond the universe. All that was, is and ever will be is the universe, which is self-sustaining.

Atonement theologically speaks of God's acting in human history to reestablish the original relationship between God and man by dealing with sin. To atone means to make amends--to repair a wrong done. Biblically, it means to remove guilt of man. The Old Testament atonements offered by the high priest were temporary and a foreshadow of the real and final atonement made by Jesus. Jesus atoned for the sins of the world (**1 John 2:2**). This atonement is received by faith (**Romans 5:1; Ephesians. 2:8-9**).

Man is a sinner (**Romans 5:8**) and cannot atone for himself. Therefore, it was the love of the Father that sent Jesus (**1 John 4:10**) to die in our place (**1 Peter 3:18**) for our sins (**1 Peter 2:24**). Because of the atonement, our fellowship with God is restored (**Romans 5:10**). [136]

Biblical Authority: The Bible alone is the Authority in the Christian life.

Biblical Inspiration: It means that the Holy Spirit controlled and guided the authors of the biblical books. They wrote exactly what God wanted said. (**2 Peter 1:21, 1 Timothy 3:16**) God Breathed.

Biblical hermeneutics is the study of the principles and methods of interpreting the text of the Bible.

Biblical Inerrancy: The Bible is without error. The Bible is verbally inspired, it is infallible, it is inerrant in the manuscripts as they were originally written.
1. It is a technical phrase for the accuracy of Biblical message.
2. It affirms that what the Bible teaches on any subject it addresses is true.
3. Properly understood, the message of the Bible gives correct information (**Hebrew 2:1-4**).
Inerrancy means without error, non-errant.
In Christianity, inerrancy states that the Bible in its original documents is without error regarding facts, names, dates, and any other revealed information. Inerrancy does not extend to the copies of the Biblical manuscripts. [137]

Biblical infallibility is the belief that what the Bible says regarding matters of faith and Christian practice is wholly useful and true. It is the "belief that the Bible is completely trustworthy as a guide to salvation and the life of faith and will not fail to accomplish its purpose. Some equate 'inerrancy' and 'infallibility'; others do not."

Biblical Inspiration: What is meant by Biblical Inspiration? It means that the Holy Spirit controlled and

---

[136] https://carm.org/dictionary-atonement (April 8, 2017)
[137] https://carm.org/dictionary-inerrancy (May 21, 2017)

guided the authors of the biblical books. They wrote exactly what God wanted said. (**2 Peter 1:21, 1 Timothy 3:16**). The Bible Incapable of mistake.

BLASPHEMY—In the sense of speaking evil of God this word is found in Ps. 74:18; Isa. 52:5; Rom. 2:24; Rev. 13:1, 6; 16:9, 11, 21. It denotes also any kind of calumny, or evil-speaking, or abuse (1 Kings 21:10; Acts 13:45; 18:6, etc.). Our Lord was accused of blasphemy when he claimed to be the Son of God (Matt. 26:65; comp. Matt. 9:3; Mark 2:7). They who deny his Messiahship blaspheme Jesus (Luke 22:65; John 10:36).

Blasphemy against the Holy Ghost (Matt. 12:31, 32; Mark 3:28, 29; Luke 12:10) is regarded by some as a continued and obstinate rejection of the gospel, and hence is an unpardonable sin, simply because as long as a sinner remains in unbelief he voluntarily excludes himself from pardon. **Others regard the expression as designating the sin of attributing to the power of Satan those miracles which Christ performed**, or generally those works which are the result of the Spirit's agency.[138]

> **BLASPHEMY.** The sin of consciously using derogatory language about God. Secondly, it is the "reviling," "mocking," and "slandering" of another human being (cf. Rom. 3:8; 1 Cor. 4:13; 1 Pet. 4:4). In the New Testament the Jewish Sanhedrin considered that Christ deserved the death penalty on account of his confession at his trial (Gk.blasphēméō; Matt. 26:65–66 par. Mark 14:64, Gk.blasphēmía; cf. earlier accusations, e.g., Matt. 9:3; John 10:36).[139]

Canon: The word, "canon," means "standard" or "rule." It is the list of authoritative and inspired Scriptures. Different religions have different canons.[140]

---

[138] Easton, M. G. (1893). In Easton's Bible dictionary. New York: Harper & Brothers.
[139] Myers, A. C. (1987). In The Eerdmans Bible dictionary (p. 162). Grand Rapids, MI: Eerdmans.
[140] https://carm.org/what-canon (May 21, 2017)

Canonization:
a. Process of declaring a person to be a saint.
b. Process by which the Scriptures were established by God and recognized in the Church; the process of determining the New Testament canon.

Christology: The word "Christology" comes from two Greek words meaning "Christ / Messiah" and "word" - which combine to mean "the study of Christ." Christology is the study of the Person and work of Jesus Christ.[141] Some of the issues studied are: His deity, His incarnation, His offices, His sacrifice, His resurrection, His teaching, His relation to God and man, and His return to earth.

Codex Sinaiticus, also known as "Aleph" (the Hebrew letter א), was found by Count Tischendorf in 1859 at the Monastery of St Catherine on Mount Sinai. Portions of the manuscript were found in the monastery dump, and a larger portion was presented to Tischendorf by one of the monks. It is a large codex, with 400 pages (or leaves) comprising about half of the Old Testament in the Septuagint version and the full New Testament.

- It has been dated to the second half of the 4th century and has been highly valued by Bible scholars in their efforts to reconstruct the original Biblical text.
- Sinaiticus has heavily influenced the translation work of modern Bible versions. Though it is considered by some scholars to represent an original form of the text, it is also recognized as the most heavily corrected early New Testament manuscript.

Codex Vaticanus, also known as "B," was found in the Vatican library. It is comprised of 759 leaves and has almost all of the Old and New Testaments. It is not known when it arrived at the Vatican, but it was included in a

---

[141] https://www.gotquestions.org/Christology.html (April 8, 2017)

catalog listing in 1475, and it is dated to the middle of the 4th century.

- Vaticanus was first used as a source document by Erasmus in his work on the "Textus Receptus." Because he viewed the text of Vaticanus to be erratic, he seldom followed it when it differed from other Greek texts.

[*Two of the oldest complete (or nearly complete) manuscripts are the* **Codex Sinaiticus** *and* **Codex Vaticanus**. They are both written on parchment, and have a large number of corrections written over the original text.] [142]

Cognitive Dissonance: is the mental discomfort (psychological stress) experienced by a person who simultaneously holds two or more contradictory beliefs, ideas, or values. The occurrence of cognitive dissonance is consequence of a person's performing an action that contradicts personal beliefs, ideals, and values; and also **occurs when confronted with new information that contradicts said beliefs, ideals, and values**.[143]

Communicable Attributes: Many attributes of God can be classified under this heading, although it is sometimes difficult to say which Biblical references to God should be regarded as attributes. A rich diversity of terminology is found in Scripture, with many synonyms. For convenience the communicable attributes are often classified as **intellectual, moral, and volitional**.   Elwell, W. A., & Beitzel, B. J. (1988). Baker encyclopedia of the Bible (878). Grand Rapids, Mich.: Baker Book House.
Classifying the attributes of God has been a topic of discussion for quite some time. Reformed theology has historically distinguished between "**Incommunicable**" and "**Communicable**" attributes of God. **Incommunicable** has been understood as attributes that only God has, while

---

[142] https://www.gotquestions.org/Codex-Sinaiticus-Vaticanus.html (May 16, 2017)
[143] https://en.wikipedia.org/wiki/Cognitive_dissonance (May 28, 2017)

Communicable attributes are those that humans possess to a degree. [144]

Deism (/ˈdiː.ɪzəm/[1][2] or /ˈdeɪ.ɪzəm/), derived from the Latin word "Deus" meaning "God", is a theological /philosophical position that combines the rejection of revelation and authority as a source of religious knowledge with the conclusion that reason and observation of the natural world are sufficient to determine the existence of a single creator of the universe.

- Belief in the existence of a God on the evidence of reason and nature only, with rejection of supernatural revelation (distinguished from theism).
- Belief in a God who created the world but has since remained indifferent to it.

Docetism was a Gnostic heresy that was condemned by the Early Church with several variations concerning the nature of Christ. Generally, it taught that Jesus only appeared to have a body and that He was not really incarnate (Greek, "dokeo" = "to seem"). This error developed out of the dualistic philosophy which viewed matter as inherently evil and that God could not be associated with matter and that God, being perfect and infinite, could not suffer.[145]

Ecclesiology is the study of the Christian church, its structure, order, practices, and hierarchy.

Eschatology is the study of the teachings in the Bible concerning the end times or of the period of time dealing with the return of Christ and the events that follow. Eschatological subjects include:

- the Resurrection,
- the Rapture,
- the Tribulation,
- the Millennium,

---

[144] https://carm.org/communicable-incommunicable-attributes-of-god (May 16, 2017
[145] https://carm.org/dictionary-docetism (April 8, 2017)

- the Binding of Satan,
- the Three witnesses,
- the Final Judgment,
- Armageddon,
- and The New Heavens and the New Earth.

In the New Testament, eschatological chapters include **Matt. 24, Mark 13, Luke 17, and 2 Thess. 2**.

In one form or another most of the books of the Bible deal with end times subjects. But some that are more prominently eschatological are Daniel, Ezekiel, Isaiah, Joel, Zechariah, Matthew, Mark, Luke, 2 Thessalonians, and of course Revelation.

(See Amillennialism and Premillennialism for more information on views on the millennium).

Eisegesis is when a person interprets and reads information into the text that is not there. [146]

Excommunication is an institutional act of religious censure used to deprive, suspend, or limit membership in a religious community.

Exegesis is when a person interprets a text based solely on what it says. That is, he extracts out of the text what is there as opposed to reading into it what is not there (Compare with Eisegesis). [147]

Gnostic Gospels: Found in Nagamadi Egypt in 1945. Written about the middle of the 3nd century – well after the so called author died. These Gnostic gospels are often pointed to as supposed "lost books of the Bible."

Hamartiology is the study of the doctrine of sin. It encompasses topics, such as The Fall of Adam and Eve, degrees of sin, original sin, and human accountability for sin.

---

[146] https://carm.org/dictionary-eisegesis (April 7, 2017)
[147] https://carm.org/dictionary-exegesis (April 7, 2017)

Henotheism: (Greek εἷς θεός heis theos "one god") is a term coined by Max Müller, to mean devotion to a single "God" while accepting the existence of other gods.

a. Müller stated that henotheism means "monotheism in principle and a polytheism in fact."

b. He made the term a center of his criticism of Western theological and religious exceptionalism (relative to Eastern religions), focusing on a cultural dogma which held "monotheism" to be both fundamentally well-defined and inherently superior to differing conceptions of God.

c. Worships one God but believes in many gods.

Hermeneutics is the Art and Science of Biblical interpretation. Theologically and Biblically speaking, it is the means by which a person examines the Bible to determine what it means.[148],[149]

Historical Revisionism identifies the re-interpretation of the historical record, of the orthodox views about a historical event, of the evidence of the event, and of the motivations and decisions of the participant people. The revision of the historical record is to reflect the contemporary discoveries of fact, evidence, and interpretation, which produce a revised history.

Homologoumena: (Greek "homologeo", means "confessed and undisputed.") These books were received as canonical without dispute, and whose right to a place in the Canon was not afterwards disputed.

Hypostatic Union:[150] This is the union of the two natures (Divine and human) in the person of Jesus. Jesus is God in flesh (John 1:1, 14, 10:30-33, 20:28, Phil. 2:5-8, Heb. 1:8). He is fully God and fully man (Col. 2:9), thus, He has two natures: God and man. He is not half God and half man. He is 100% God and 100% man. He never lost His divinity. He continued to exist as God when He became a

---

[148] https://carm.org/dictionary-hermeneutics (April 8, 2017)
[149] https://www.gotquestions.org/Biblical-hermeneutics.html (April 8, 2017)
[150] https://www.gotquestions.org/hypostatic-union.html (April 8, 2017)

man and added human nature to Himself (Phil. 2:5-11). Therefore, there is a "union in one person of a full human nature and a full divine nature." Right now in Heaven there is a man, Jesus, who is our Mediator between us and God the Father (1 Tim. 2:5).[151]

Hypostasis is a Greek word ὑπόστασις that has a range of meanings: nature, substance, image, essence, etc. It is translated as "nature" in the NASB in Heb. 1:3, "And He is the radiance of His glory and the exact representation of His nature, and upholds all things by the word of His power." It is translated as "image" in the ASV, KJV and NKJV, "imprint" in the ESV and NRSV. It is also found in

- 2 Cor. 9:4, "otherwise if any Macedonians come with me and find you unprepared, we--not to speak of you--will be put to shame by this confidence [hypostasis]," (NASB).
- Heb. 3:14, "For we have become partakers of Christ, if we hold fast the beginning of our assurance [hypostasis] firm until the end," (NASB).
- Heb. 11:1, "Now faith is the assurance [hypostasis] of things hoped for, the conviction of things not seen," (NASB).

It is borrowed for the English term Hypostatic Union which is the teaching that in the one person of Christ are two natures.[152]

Illumination: To enlighten or to make to/give understanding. This is different from Revelation which reveals a truth. God makes known (reveals) a truth and the Holy Spirit makes to understand (illuminates) that truth. In Daniel 7th chapter: he is given a vision (revelation) but does not understand it. Starting at verse 15 he asked and gets the understanding (illumination) of the truth he had received. In Revelation John receives revelation through visions and the Angel of the Lord

---

[151] https://carm.org/dictionary-hypostatic-union (April 8, 2017)
[152] https://carm.org/dictionary-hypostasis (April 9, 2017)

Illuminated the truth. Also see **Daniel 8:15-17. 1 Corinthians 2:11-12; Ephesians 1:17-18; 1 John 2:20**. The process by which God enlightens a person's mind so that he understands the significance of the objective disclosure of God (revelation) for his life subjectively.

Impassibility (from Latin in-, "not", passibilis, "able to suffer, experience emotion") describes the theological doctrine that God does not experience pain or pleasure from the actions of another being.
It has often been seen as a consequence of divine aseity, the idea that God is absolutely independent of any other being, i.e., in no way causally dependent. Being affected (literally made to have a certain emotion, affect) by the state or actions of another would seem to imply causal dependence. [153]

Impeccable: faultless; flawless; irreproachable: *impeccable manners.*
Impeccability, when speaking of God, means the inability to sin. Christ was impeccable in that He could not sin and He did not sin (1 Peter 2:22). There is dispute as to whether or not Jesus could have sinned since He was a man as well as divine. But Jesus, the person, claimed the attributes of both divinity and humanity (see Communicatio Idiomatum). That is, He knew all things, could forgive sins, etc., but also was hungry and had to sleep. Since the divine attributes as well as the human attributes were ascribed to Jesus and the divine attribute means that God cannot sin, it is logical to conclude that Jesus could not have sinned.

Peccablity: liable to sin or error.

Kashrut (also kashruth or kashrus, כַּשְׁרוּת) is a set of Jewish religious dietary laws. Food that may be consumed according to halakha (Jewish law) is termed kosher /ˈkoʊʃər/ in English, from the Ashkenazi pronunciation of

---

[153] https://en.wikipedia.org/wiki/Impassibility (May 21, 2017)

the Hebrew term kashér (כָּשֵׁר), meaning "fit" (in this context, fit for consumption).[154]

Kiddush (/ˈkɪdɪʃ/; Hebrew: קידוש [kiˈduʃ]), literally, "sanctification," is a blessing recited over wine or grape juice to sanctify the Shabbat and Jewish holidays. Additionally, the word refers to a small repast held on Shabbat or festival mornings after the prayer services and before the meal.[155]

Kosher foods are those that conform to the regulations of kashrut (Jewish dietary law). Food that may be consumed according to halakha (Jewish law) is termed kosher (pronunciation: /koʊʃər/) in English, from the Ashkenazi pronunciation of the Hebrew term kashér (כָּשֵׁר, pronunciation: /kɑːʃɛər/), meaning "fit" (in this context, fit for consumption). Food that is not in accordance with Jewish law is called treif (Yiddish: טרייף, pronunciation: /treɪf/, derived from Hebrew: טְרֵפָה trāfáh) meaning "torn."[156]

Modalism, also called **Sabellianism,** is the unorthodox belief that God is one person who has revealed himself in three forms or *modes* in contrast to the Trinitarian doctrine where God is one being eternally existing in three persons.[157,158]

Monarchianism (mono--"one"; arche--"rule") was an error concerning the nature of God that developed in the second century A.D. Modal Monarchianism teaches that the Father, the Son, and the Holy Spirit are just modes of the single person who is God. In other words, the Father, Son, and Holy Spirit are not simultaneous and separate persons but consecutive modes of one person. Churches. However, the present-day modalists maintain that God's name is Jesus. They also require baptism "in Jesus' name"

[154] https://en.wikipedia.org/wiki/Kashrut (May 1, 2017)
[155] https://en.wikipedia.org/wiki/Kiddush (May 1, 2017)
[156] https://en.wikipedia.org/wiki/Kosher_foods (May 1, 2017)
[157] https://carm.org/dictionary-modalism (April 9, 2017)
[158] https://www.gotquestions.org/Sabellianism-Modalism-Monarchianism.html (April 9, 2017)

not "in the name of the Father, the Son, and the Holy Spirit" for salvation.[159]

Monogenes - The phrase "only begotten" translates the Greek word monogenes. This word is variously translated into English as "only," "one and only," and "only begotten."

Monotheism is the belief in a single all-powerful god, as opposed to religions that believe in multiple gods. Judaism, Christianity, and Islam are widely practiced forms of *monotheism*.[160]

> ***Monotheism:*** In theology, monotheism (from Greek μόνος "one" and θεός "god") is the belief in the existence of one deity or God, or in the oneness of God.[1] In a Western context, the concept of "monotheism" tends to be dominated by the concept of the God of the Abrahamic religions and the Platonic concept of God as put forward by Pseudo-Dionysius the Areopagite.

Monism: Monism is a philosophical worldview in which all of reality can be reduced to one "thing" or "substance." This view is opposed to dualism(in which all of reality is reducible to two substances, e.g., good and evil; light and darkness; form and matter; body and soul) and pluralism (all of reality is comprised of multiple substances). In all of these philosophical views, this article uses the word *substance* in a technical sense to mean "essence," or its "thing-ishness"; in other words, something in which properties adhere. ***All existence is one substance (like rain drops in the sea).***

Muratorian Canon (also called the Muratorian Fragment) is an ancient list of New Testament books—the oldest such list we have found.

The original document, which was probably written in Greek, is dated to about AD 180 and lists 22 of the 27

---

books that were later included in the New Testament of the Christian Bible.[161]

Orthodoxy: a belief or a way of thinking that is accepted as true or correct. Orthodoxy is the belief in the standards of accepted and true doctrines taught in the Bible. That which is orthodox agrees with Biblical teaching and the interpretation of the Christian Church. False religions are not orthodox. They are heterodox.[162]

Pantheism: Pantheism views God as being active in the universe but not beyond the universe.
  a. In fact, God is seen as being the universe. There is no creation and Creator, only one reality.
  b. God is everything and everything is God.
  c. Pantheism is found in forms of Hinduism, Zen Buddhism and Christian Science. It is very prevalent among eastern religions. All or everything is God.

Pan-en-theism: this view says God is in the universe and is growing to achieve his potential beyond the universe. It is similar to finite godism in that it views God as limited, but it is different in the sense that God is potentially infinite as he develops. God is in everything bringing it to fruition.

PHARISEES [făr´ə sēz] **(Gk. Pharisaíoi).†** One of the parties or movements within Judaism of the late Second Temple period (ca. 150 B.C.-A.D. 70). **The Pharisees were noted most for their exact observance of the Jewish religion**, their accurate exposition of the law, their handing down of extrabiblical customs and traditions, their moderate position with regard to the interplay of fate and free will, and their belief in the coming resurrection and in angels (Josephus BJ i.5.2 [110]; ii.8.14 [162–63]; Ant. xiii.10.6 [297]; xviii.1.3 [13–14]; Mark 7:3; Acts 23:6–9; Phil. 3:5; cf. Gal. 1:14). **The ancient sources variously describe the Pharisees as a political party, a philosophical school and scholarly class, or a sect or**

---

[161] https://www.gotquestions.org/Muratorian-Canon.html (May 16, 2017)
[162] https://carm.org/dictionary-orthodoxy (April 7, 2017)

voluntary association (Heb. ḥaberôt devoted to ritual purity.[163]

Pneumatology: The study of the Holy Spirit, His person, works, relation to the Father and Son, relation to man, ministry in salvation and sanctification, conviction, and indwelling.

Polytheism: Polytheism believes that there are many finite gods in the world who actively influence the world. They are unlike theism in that there is no infinite God. They are unlike deism in that there is supernatural activity in the world. They are unlike finite godism in that there is no God beyond the universe. Some pantheists are also polytheists in that many gods are representative expressions of the god that is everything. Many people throughout the world are polytheistic, most notably modern Mormons. The ancient Greeks of the days of the New Testament were polytheists.

Process-Theism: Process theists, in contrast, maintain that God and the basic material out of which the rest of reality is composed are coeternal. Moreover, process theists believe that all actual entities always possess some degree of self-determination.
   a. God, it is held, does present to every actual entity at every moment the best available course of action. And each entity does feel some compulsion to act in accordance with this divine lure.
   b. But process theists deny that God possesses the capacity to control unilaterally the activity of any entity. Thus, what occurs in relation to every aspect of reality involving a multiplicity of entities – for example, what happens in relation to every earthly state of affairs – is always a cooperative effort.

---

[163] Myers, A. C. (1987). In The Eerdmans Bible dictionary (p. 823). Grand Rapids, MI: Eerdmans.

Pseudepigrapha: falsely attributed works, texts whose claimed author is represented by a separate author, or a work "whose real author attributed it to a figure of the past". The word *pseudepigrapha* (from the **Greek**: ψευδής, *pseudes*, "false" and ἐπιγραφή, *epigraphē*, "name" or "inscription" or "ascription"; thus when taken together it means "false superscription or title"; see the related *epigraphy*) is the plural of "pseudepigraphon" (sometimes Latinized as "pseudepigraphum").

Redemption means to free someone from bondage. It often involves the paying of a ransom, a price that makes redemption possible. The Israelites were redeemed from Egypt. We were redeemed from the power of sin and the curse of the Law **(Galatians 3:13)** through Jesus **(Romans 3:24, Colossians 1:14)**. We were bought with a price **(1 Corinthians 6:20, 7:23)**.[164]

Replacement Theology is the teaching that the Christian church has replaced Israel regarding God's purpose and promises.

Revelation: Term from the Latin revelatio, referring to either the act of revealing or making known, or the thing which is revealed. In theology it designates God's own self-disclosure or manifesting of himself, or things concerning himself and the world; it may also mean the word itself, oral or written, which bears such revelation. The equivalent NT terms are apokalupsis (apocalypse), which means unveiling, uncovering, or making someone or something known. It can also mean the word itself which reveals. There is a strong emphasis on the revelation of God by God as the source of Christian doctrine. Natural theology states that knowledge of God can be gained through a combination of observation of nature and human reason.

---

[164] https://carm.org/dictionary-redemption (April 8, 2017)

SCRIBES (Heb. sōperîm; Gk. grammateis, nomikoi (lawyers) and nomodidaskaloi (teachers of the law)). Scribes were experts in the study of the law of Moses (Torah). At first this occupation belonged to the priests. Ezra was priest and scribe (Ne. 8:9); the offices were not necessarily separate. The chief activity of the scribe was undistracted study (Ecclus. 38:24). The rise of the scribes may be dated after the Babylonian Exile. 1 Ch. 2:55 would suggest that the scribes were banded together into families and guilds. Scribes were found in Rome in the later imperial period, and in Babylonia in the 5th and 6th centuries AD. Not until about AD 70 are there detailed facts concerning individual scribes. They were mainly influential in Judaea up to AD 70, but they were to be found in Galilee (Lk. 5:17) and among the Dispersion.

The scribes were the originators of the synagogue service. Some of them sat as members of the Sanhedrin (Mt. 16:21; 26:3). After AD 70 the importance of the scribes was enhanced. They preserved in written form the oral law and faithfully handed down the Heb. Scriptures. They expected of their pupils a reverence beyond that given to parents (Aboth 4. 12).

The function of the scribes was threefold.

1. **They preserved the law**. They transmitted unwritten legal decisions which had come into existence in their efforts to apply the Mosaic law to daily life. They claimed this oral law was more important than the written law (Mk. 7:5ff.). By their efforts religion was liable to be reduced to heartless formalism.

2. **They gathered around them many pupils to instruct them in the law**. The pupils were expected to retain the material taught and to

transmit it without variation. They lectured in the Temple (Lk. 2:46; Jn. 18:20).

3. **They were referred to as 'lawyers' and 'teachers of the law', because they were entrusted with the administration of the law as judges in the Sanhedrin** (cf. Mt. 22:35; Mk. 14:43, 53; Lk. 22:66; Acts 4:5; Jos., Ant. 18.16f.). 'Lawyer' and 'scribe' are synonymous, and thus the two words are never joined in the NT

The **OT Apocrypha and Pseudepigrapha are sources for the origin of the scribal party**. The books of Ezra, Nehemiah, Daniel, Chronicles and Esther also indicate something of the beginnings of the movement, whereas Josephus and the NT speak of this group in a more advanced stage of development. There is no mention of the scribes in the Fourth Gospel. They belonged mainly to the party of the Pharisees, but as a body were distinct from them. On the matter of the resurrection they sided with Paul against the Sadducees (Acts 23:9). They clashed with Christ, for he taught with authority (Mt. 7:28–29), and he condemned external formalism which they fostered. **They persecuted Peter and John** (Acts 4:5), and had a part in Stephen's martyrdom (Acts 6:12). However, although the majority opposed Christ (Mt. 21:15), some believed (Mt. 8:19).[165]

SADDUCEES [săd´ōō sēz] (Gk. Saddoukaioi; from Heb. ṣeḏûqîm). **A party existing within Judaism from some time in the second century B.C. to the war of A.D. 66–70.** The name came most likely from that of Zadok, the high priest of David's day from whom the high priests were descended. (The alternate derivation of "Sadducees" from

[165] Feinberg, C. L. (1996). Scribes. In D. R. W. Wood, I. H. Marshall, A. R. Millard, J. I. Packer, & D. J. Wiseman (Eds.), New Bible dictionary (3rd ed., pp. 1068–1069). Leicester, England; Downers Grove, IL: InterVarsity Press.

a later Zadok, a disciple of Antigonus of Soko, is late and not trustworthy.) **The Sadducees did, indeed, favor the priests and accord them an elevated role in their interpretation of the law.** By the time of **Jesus they included the families who supplied the high priests, as well as other wealthy aristocrats of Jerusalem**. Most members of the Sanhedrin, the central judicial authority of Jewish people, were Sadducees. Thus **the Sadducees were the party of those with political power, those allied with the Herodian and Roman rulers**, but they were not a group with influence among the people themselves. The views of the Pharisees prevailed among the common people, so that even though the two groups differed with regard to items in the laws of purity and details of temple procedure during the feasts, the Saducean priests were compelled to operate according to the Pharisees' views.

The differences between the two parties were not merely concentrated on a few details, but extended to their social standing (few Pharisees being aristocrats) and to the very principles by which they answered religious questions. **The Sadducees accepted only the written Torah and rejected all "oral Torah,"** i.e., the traditional interpretation of the Torah accepted by the Pharisees that became of central importance in rabbinic Judaism. Scholars once held that the Sadducees accepted only the Pentateuch and not the prophets. Such was apparently not the case, although the Sadducees may have weighted their use of the canon toward the Pentateuch. They rejected the doctrine of the future resurrection, belief in angels and spirits as it generally developed in postbiblical Judaism, and the predestinarian views held by the Pharisees. The Sadducees represented in these ways a conservatism that limited both the acceptance of religious ideas not represented in the old sources and the interpretation of every aspect of life by reference to religion, which is precisely what the Pharisees most sought.[166]

Shema: the Jewish confession of faith made up of Deuteronomy 6:4–9 and 11:13–21 and Numbers 15:37–41.

Soteriology is the study of the doctrine of salvation. It is derived from the Greek word, soterious, which means salvation. Some of the subjects of soteriology are the atonement, imputation, and regeneration.

Synoptic: presenting or taking the same or common view; specifically, often capitalized: of or relating to the first three Gospels of the New Testament [Matthew, Mark, Luke]

Tetragrammaton (from Greek Τετραγράμματον, meaning "[consisting of] four letters") is the Hebrew theonym יהוה, commonly transliterated into Latin letters as YHWH. It is one of the names of God used in the Hebrew Bible. The name may be derived from a verb that means "to be", "to exist", "to cause to become", or "to come to pass". [167]

Textus Receptus (Latin for "Received Text") is a Greek New Testament that provided the textual base for the vernacular translations of the Reformation Period.
 • **It was a printed tex**t, not a hand-copied manuscript, **created in the 15th century to fill the need for a textually accurate Greek New Testamen**t.
Erasmus, a 15th-century Dutch theologian, working at great speed in order to beat to press another Greek New Testament being prepared in Spain, gathered together what hand-copied Greek manuscripts he could locate. He found five or six, the majority of which were dated in the

---

[166] Myers, A. C. (1987). In The Eerdmans Bible dictionary (p. 902). Grand Rapids, MI: Eerdmans.
[167] https://en.wikipedia.org/wiki/Tetragrammaton (May 16, 2017)

twelfth century. Working with all the speed he could, Erasmus did not even transcribe the manuscripts; he merely made notes on the manuscripts themselves and sent them to the printers. The entire New Testament was printed in about six to eight months and published in 1516. It became a best seller, despite its errors, and the first printing was soon gone. A second edition was published in 1519 with some of the errors having been corrected.

Erasmus published two other editions in 1527 and 1535. Stung by criticism that his work contained numerous textual errors, he incorporated readings from the Greek New Testament published in Spain in later editions of his work. Erasmus' Greek text became the standard in the field, and other editors and printers continued the work after his death in 1536. In 1633, another edition was published. In the publisher's preface, in Latin, we find these words: "Textum ergo habes, nun cab omnibus receptum," which can be translated as "the [reader] now has the text that is received by all." From that publisher's notation have come the words "Received Text."

- The Textus Receptus became the dominant Greek text of the New Testament for the following two hundred and fifty years.
- It was not until the publication of the Westcott and Hort Greek New Testament in 1881 that the Textus Receptus lost its position.[168]

Textual criticism is a method used to determine what the original manuscripts of the Bible said.

- The original manuscripts of the Bible are either lost, hidden, or no longer in existence.
- What we do have is tens of thousands of copies of the original manuscripts dating from the 1st to the 15th centuries A.D. (for the New Testament) and dating from the 4th century B.C. to the 15th century A.D. (for the Old Testament). In these manuscripts, there are many minor and a few somewhat major differences.

---

[168] https://www.gotquestions.org/Textus-Receptus.html (May 16, 2017)

- Textual criticism is the study of these manuscripts in an attempt to determine what the original reading actually was.

There are three primary methods to textual criticism.

1 The first is the **Textus Receptus**. The Textus Receptus was a manuscript of the Bible that was compiled by a man named Erasmus in the 1500s A.D. He took the limited number of manuscripts he had access to and compiled them into what eventually became known as the Textus Receptus. The Textus Receptus is the textual basis behind the King James Version and New King James Version.

2 A second method is known as the **Majority Text.** The Majority Text takes all of the manuscripts that are available today, compares the differences, and chooses the most likely correct reading based on which reading occurs the most. For example, if 748 manuscripts read "he said" and 1429 manuscripts read "they said" - the Majority Text will go with "they said" as the most likely original reading. There are no major Bible translations that are based on the Majority Text.

3 The third method is known as the **critical or eclectic method**. The eclectic method involves considering external and internal evidences for determining the most likely original text. External evidence makes us ask these questions: in how many manuscripts does the reading occur? what are the dates for these manuscripts? in what region of the world were these manuscripts found? Internal evidence prompts these questions: what could have caused these varying readings? which reading can possibly explain the origin of the other readings? The New International Version, New American Standard, New Living Translation, and most other Bible translations use the Eclectic Text.[169]

The Immutability of God is an attribute where "God is unchanging in his character, will, and covenant promises."

---

[169] https://www.gotquestions.org/textual-criticism.html (May 16, 2017)

The Majority Text, also known as the Byzantine and Ecclesiastical Text, is a method of determining the original reading of a Scripture by discovering what reading occurs in a majority of the manuscripts. As the Greek New Testament was copied hundreds of times over 1500 years, the scribes, as careful as they were, occasionally made mistakes. The vast majority of these mistakes are in misspellings, or in whether "the" or a preposition occurs. It is important to remember, though, that no doctrine of the Christian faith is put into doubt by these textual questions. The testimony of the thousands of manuscripts over 1500 years is entirely consistent on all the key issues of the Christian faith.

It is vital, though, that our Bibles are as accurate as possible. The accuracy of the manuscripts plays a large role in determining the accuracy of the translation. While the presence of a *the* is not usually vital to the meaning of a verse, there are times when it can be. This is where the science of "textual criticism" comes in. The goal of textual criticism is to examine all of the available manuscripts, and by comparison and contrast, to determine what the original text truly was.

The Majority Text method within textual criticism could be called the "democratic" method. Essentially, each Greek manuscript has one vote, all the variants are voted on by all the manuscripts, and whichever variant has the most votes wins. At first glance, the Majority Text method would seem to be the most likely to result in the correct original reading. The problem is that the Majority Text method does not take into account two very important factors: (1) The age of the manuscripts, and (2) the location of the manuscripts.[170]

Theology: The word, theology, comes from two Greek words, theos (God) and logos (word) that combined mean "the study of God". Christian theology is simply an attempt to understand God as He is revealed in the Bible. No theology will ever fully explain God and His ways because

---

[170] https://www.gotquestions.org/majority-text.html (May 16, 2017)

God is infinitely and eternally higher than we are. Therefore, any attempt to describe Him will fall short (**Romans 11:33-36**).[171] God is the single supreme being in all the universe. He has such attributes as omniscience (all-knowing, 1 John 3:20), omnipresence (existing everywhere, Psalm 139:7-12), and omnipotence (He accomplishes whatever He desires, Jer. 32:17, 27). He is eternal (Psalm 90:2), holy (Isaiah 6:3), merciful (Psalm 67:1), and gracious (1 Pet. 2:3). All these things we discover about God from the Bible. Therefore, theology is very important because in it we can discover who and what God is and what He desires for us (1 Cor. 1:9).[172]

Theology Proper is the sub-discipline of Systematic Theology which deals specifically with the being, attributes and works of God.

Trinity: The word "trinity" is a term used to denote the Christian doctrine that God exists as a unity of three distinct persons: Father, Son, and Holy Spirit. Each of the persons is distinct from the other yet identical in essence. In other words, each is fully divine in nature, but each is not the totality of the other persons of the Trinity. Each has a will, loves, and says "I" and "You" when speaking. The Father is not the same person as the Son, who is not the same person as the Holy Spirit, and who is not the same person as the Father. Each is divine, yet there are not three gods but one God. There are three individual subsistences or persons. The word "subsistence" means something that has a real existence. The word "person" denotes individuality and self-awareness. The Trinity is three of these though the latter term has become the dominant one used to describe the individual aspects of God known as the Father, the Son, and the Holy Spirit.[173]

References on the Trinity:

Theology and Doctrine, Charts of Christian by H Wayne House; Zondervan pg. 43.

---

[171] https://www.gotquestions.org/what-is-theology.html (**May 28, 2017**)
[172] https://carm.org/questions/about-doctrine/what-theology (May 28, 2017)
[173] https://carm.org/what-trinity (April 9, 2017)

Church History, Charts of Ancient and Medieval by John D. Hannah; Zondervan pg. 63.

Theology and Doctrine, Charts of Christian by H Wayne House; Zondervan pg. 44.

Church History, Charts of Ancient and Medieval by John D. Hannah; Zondervan pg. 61.

Theology and Doctrine, Charts of Christian by H Wayne House; Zondervan pg. 44.

Church History Charts of Ancient and Medieval by John D. Hannah; Zondervan pg. 71.

Church History Chronological and Background charts; Zonervan, Robert C. Walton. Pg. 25.

Theology and Doctrine charts of Christian by H. Wayne House; Zondervan pg 44.

Church History Chronological and Background charts; Zonervan, Robert C. Walton. Pg. 26.

Church History charts of Ancient and Medieval by John D. Hannah; Zondervan pg 70.

Church History charts of Ancient and Medieval by John D. Hannah; Zondervan pg 73.

Church History charts of Ancient and Medieval by John D. Hannah; Zondervan pg 72.

https://en.wikipedia.org/wiki/Nestorianism (12/13/2016)
https://en.wikipedia.org/wiki/Monothelitism (12/13/2016)
https://en.wikipedia.org/wiki/Tritheism (12/14/2016)
https://www.vocabulary.com/dictionary/polemicist (12/13/2016)
https://orthodoxwiki.org/Theophilus_of_Antioch (12/14/2016)
https://en.wikipedia.org/wiki/Theophilus_of_Antioch (12/14/2016)
https://en.wikipedia.org/wiki/Tertullian 12/14/2016
https://en.wikipedia.org/wiki/Third_Council_of_Constantinople (12/14/2016)
https://en.wikipedia.org/wiki/Second_Council_of_Nicaea (12/14/2016)
https://www.ccel.org/creeds/athanasian.creed.html (12/13/2016)
https://en.wikipedia.org/wiki/Eutychianism (12/13/2016)
https://en.wikipedia.org/wiki/Arianism (12/13/2016
https://www.britannica.com/topic/Macedonianism (12/13/2016
https://en.wikipedia.org/wiki/Monarchianism 912/14/2016)
https://en.wikipedia.org/wiki/Unitarianism (12/14/2016)
https://en.wikipedia.org/wiki/Sabellianism (12/14/2016)
https://en.wikipedia.org/wiki/Council_of_Ephesus (12/15/2016)
https://en.wikipedia.org/wiki/Council_of_Chalcedon (12/14/2016)
https://en.wikipedia.org/wiki/Second_Council_of_Constantinople (12/14/2016)
https://en.wikipedia.org/wiki/Trinitarianism_in_the_Church_Fathers
https://en.wikipedia.org/wiki/Apollinarism (12/13/2016)

Universalism is the teaching that all people will be saved. Some say that it is through the atonement of Jesus that all will ultimately be reconciled to God. Others just say that all will go to Heaven sooner or later whether or not they have trusted in or rejected Jesus as Savior during their lifetime. This universal redemption will be realized in the future where God will bring all people to repentance. This repentance can happen while a person lives or after he has died and lived again in the millennium (as some "Christian universalists" claim) or some future state. Additionally, a few universalists even maintain that Satan and all demons will likewise be reconciled to God.[174]

---

[174] https://carm.org/universalism-is (May 21, 2017)

COMPARISONS

Anthropomorphic is defined as manifesting in human form. It is from the Greek "anthropos" meaning "man" and "morphe" meaning "form." In Biblical theology, **God is described in anthropomorphic terms**, that is, in human terms with human attributes. For example, God has hands and feet in Exodus 24:9-11 and is loving (1 John 4:8).

> *"4 The Lord is in his holy temple, the Lord's throne is in heaven: **his eyes** behold, **his eyelids** try, the children of men."* (**Psalms 11:4**)

Metaphor: When the comparison is direct, and one thing is called another, without like or as, it is a metaphor. This is a very popular device:

> *"For the Lord God is a sun and shield: the Lord will give grace and glory: no good thing will he withhold from them that walk uprightly."* (**Psalms 84:11**)
> *"A garden enclosed is my sister, my spouse; a spring shut up, a fountain sealed."* (**Song of Songs 4:12**)

Personification: the attribution of human nature or character to animals, inanimate objects, or abstract notions, especially as a rhetorical figure.

An object or **abstract quality is treated as a person**:

> *"11 Let the heavens **rejoice**, and let the earth be **glad;** Let the sea roar, and all its fullness; 12 Let the field be **joyful**, and all that is in it. Then all the trees of the woods **will rejoice** before the Lord"* (**Psalms 96:11, 12**).

> *"I wisdom dwell with prudence, and find out knowledge of witty inventions."* (**Proverbs 8:12**)

Simile: When the comparison uses the word **"like"** or **"as"** it is called a **simile**:

*"12 For thou, Lord, wilt bless the righteous; with favour wilt thou compass him **as** with a shield." (**Psalms 5:12**)*

"**As** the apple tree among the trees of the wood, so is my beloved among the sons." (**Song of Songs 2:3a**)

*"His head and his hairs were white **like** wool, **as** white **as** snow; and his eyes were **as** a flame of fire;"* (**Revelation 1:14**)

Zoomorphism: Similarly, God's attributes are compared to animal forms:

*"He shall cover thee with **his feathers**, and under **his wings** shalt thou trust: his truth shall be thy shield and buckler."* (**Psalms 91:4**)

THEOLOGICAL ARGUMENTS

1. **Cosmological Argument**: Every event has a cause. The universe had a beginning. Therefore, the universe has a cause

2. **Teleological Argument**: Design implies a designer, The universe manifests design, Therefore, the universe has a designer

3. **Ontological Argument**: A necessary being is by definition one that cannot not exist. But what cannot not exist, must exist. Therefore, a necessary being must exist.

4. **Anthropological** Argument: Man is an intelligent being - Only intelligence can produce the intelligent - Therefore, an Intelligent Being created man

5. **Creation Ex Materia**: creatio ex materia (**creation** out of some pre-existent, eternal matter)

6. **Creation EX DEO:** creatio ex deo (**creation** out of the being of God).

7. **Creation Ex nihilo** is a Latin phrase **meaning** "out of nothing". It often appears in conjunction with the concept of **creation**, as in **creatio ex nihilo**, **meaning** "**creation** out of nothing"—chiefly in

philosophical or theological contexts, but also occurs in other fields.

RESOURCES

You will need internal (Bible) and external resources to uphold the Christian faith. The Bible is our main and primary resource, however there will be times you will need extrabiblical information in the defense and teaching of the Bible. You will learn that even enemies of the Bible can be an unknown asset.

This is not an exhaustive list, and it is presented simply as a place of recommendation to get started in growing your collection of Biblical research material. Resources as helpful as they can be, should always be verified and cross checked with other sources.

> "*Study to shew thyself approved unto God, a workman that needeth not to be ashamed, **rightly dividing the word of truth**.*" (**2 Timothy 2:15**)

> "***Prove all things***; *hold fast that which is good.*" (**1 Thessalonians 5:21**)

ONLINE RESOURCES:
   a. Non biblical accounts of New Testament events and/or people.[175]
   b. Manuscript Evidence for Superior New Testament reliability.[176]
   c. Manuscript Evidence for the Bible[177]
   d. Does the Bible provide extraordinary evidence for Jesus' Resurrection? [178]
   e. Regarding the quotes from the historian Josephus about Jesus.[179]
   f. 101 Scientific Facts & Foreknowledge.[180]
   g. Who was Constantine the Great?[181]

BIBLE RESOURCE BOOKS
A) Bible Choices

---

[175] https://carm.org/non-biblical-accounts-new-testament-events-and-or-people (May 21, 2017)
[176] https://carm.org/manuscript-evidence (May 21, 2017)
[177] http://www.faithfacts.org/search-for-truth/maps/manuscript-evidence (May 21, 2017)
[178] https://carm.org/does-bible-provide-extraordinary-evidence-jesus-resurrection (May 21, 2017)
[179] https://carm.org/regarding-quotes-historian-josephus-about-jesus (May 21, 2017)
[180] http://www.eternal-productions.org/101science.html (May 21, 2017)
[181] https://www.gotquestions.org/Constantine-the-Great.html (May 21, 2017)

a. The Apologetics Study Bible, general editor Ted Cabal
b. Life Application Study Bible – NIV
c. Comparative Study Bible – Parallel NIV, KJV, NASB AMP
d. The Expositor's Study Bible KJV/Concordance

B) Bible Commentary: should cover the following:

a. **Culture**
b. **History**
c. **Language**
d. **Evidence**
   1. The Layman's Bible Commentary In one Volume
   2. Believers Bible Commentary by William MacDonald
   3. New Bible Commentary by G.J. Wenham, J. A. Motyer, D.A. Carson, and R.T. France
   4. Nelson's Compact Series Compact Bible Handbook by George Knight

C) Bible Dictionary

Dictionary of The Bible by David Noel Freedman
Nelson's New Illustrated Bible Dictionary by R. F. Youngblood

D) Bible Customs & Manners

Nelson's New Illustrated Bible Manners & Customs by Howard F. Vos
Manners & Customs of The Bible by James M. Freemann

E) Theology Bible & Systematic

a. Systematic Theology **"An Introduction To Biblical Doctrine"** by Wayne Grudem
b. General Introduction to the Bible by Norman Geisler
c. The New Evidence That Demands A Verdict by Josh McDowell
d. Evidence for Christianity by Josh McDowell
e. The Moody HandBook of Theology by Paul Enns

F) Lexicon Greek/Hebrew
The New Strong's Expanded Exhaustive Concordance of the bible with Greek/Hebrew Dictionary.

G) Bible Concordance
Young's Analytical Concordance To The Bible

H) Church History & Apologetics
a. History of The Christian Church (volumes 1 through 8) by Philip Schaff
b. Christening The Roman Empire A.D. 100-400 by Ramsay McMullen
c. Eusebius The History of The Church by G. A. Williamson
d. The Apostolic Fathers by Jack N. Sparks
e. Baker Encyclopedia of Christian Apologetics, by Norman L. Geisler
f. The Story of Christianity by Justo L. Gonzalez
g. The Big Book of Bible Difficulties by Geisler and Howe
h. Hard sayings of the Bible by Kaiser, Davids, Bruce, Brauch
i. When Critics Ask by Geisler and Howe
j. Commonly Misunderstood Bible Verses by Ron Rhodes
k. Names of God & Other Bible Studies by Rose Publishing
l. Christianizing The Roman Empire A.D.100-400 by Ramsay MacMullen

Other Good Resource Books

1. **All The men of The Bible** by Herbert Lockyer.
2. **All The Women of The Bible** by Herbert Lockyer.
3. **The Bible in Translation by Bruce M. Metzger**
4. **A Visual History of The English Bible by Donald L. Drake**
5. What the Bible is All About by Henrietta Mears

6. **Growing Toward Spiritual Maturity** By Gary C. Newton (ETA)
7. **Understanding Teaching** "Effective Biblical Teaching by Gregory C. Carson (ETA)
8. **Bibical Beliefs By Clarence Benson (ETA)**
9. **You & Your Bible (ETA)**
10. **Old Testament Bible History** by Alfred Edersheim
11. Nelson's Pocket Series **Bible Handbook**
12. Nelson's Pocket Series **Bible People**
13. Nelson's Cross Reference Guide to The Bible by Jerome Smith
14. The New Treasury of Scripture Knowledge by Jerome Smith
15. The Ultimate Cross-Reference Treasury by Jerome Smith (E-Sword Software)
16. Where to Find it In The Bible by Ken Anderson
17. Encyclopedia of Bible Difficulties by Gleason L. Archer Jr.
18. **Handbook of Denominations in the United** States by Frank S. Mead
19. **The Popular Survey of The Old Testament by Norman Geisler**
20. **The Popular Survey of The New Testament by Norman Geisler**
21. **The Popular Handbook of Archaelogy and the Bible by Norman Geisler & Joseph M. Holden**
22. **The Works of Josephus by William Whiston**
23. Figures of Speech used in the Bible by E. W. Bullinger
24. World History :The Human Journey by Holt RineHart, and Winston
25. The Case For Christ by Lee Strobel
26. Defending Black Faith by Craig S. Keener & Glenn Usry
27. Black Man's Religion by Glenn Usry & Craig S. Keener
28. A Review of the Apostolic Faith Movement by Quintin Wingate
29. The BlueBook on Evangelism by Ray Comfort

30. Christianity in Crisis 21 Century by Hank Hanegraaff
31. The Complete Bible Answer Book by Hank Hanegraaff
32. The Bible Answer Book Volume 2 by Hank Hanegraaff
33. The Forgotten Trinity by James R. White
34. Bible Prophecy by Mark Hitchcock
35. The Word's Living Religions by Robert E. Hume
36. Meredith's Complete Book of Bible Lists by Joel L. Meredith
37. Modern Science And Christian Faith by Bernard Ramm
38. The Life and The Epistles of St. Paul by Conybeare & Howson
39. Five Minute Church Historian by Dr. Rick Cornish

BOOKS WITH CHARTS

1. Church History (Charts of Ancient and Medieval) by John D. Hannah
2. New Testament (Charts of Chronological and Background) H. Wayne House
3. Charts of Reformation and Enlightment Church History by John D. Hannah
4. Old Testament (Charts of Chronological and Background) by John H. Walton
5. Charts of Bible Prophecy by H. Wayne House & Randall Price
6. Church History (Charts of Chronological and Background) Robert C. Walton
7. Charts of Apologetics and Christian Evidences by H. Wayne House & Joseph M. Holden
8. Charts of World Religions by H. Wayne House
9. Charts of Christian Theology and Doctrine by H. Wayne House
10. Charts of Cults, Sects, and Religious Movements by H. Wayne House

Cult Apologetics Books

1. The Kingdom of the Cults by Walter Martin
2. The Kingdom of the Occult by Walter Martin
3. Correcting the Cults by Norman Geisler and Ron Rhodes
4. Christianity, Cults, and Religion by Rose Publishing
5. Handbook on Cults & New Religions by Ron Rhodes

The Quran and Books on Islam

1. Translated and Explained by Muhammad Asad
2. Translation by A. Yusuf Ali
3. The Generous Qur'an by Usama Dakdok
4. Translated by Allamah Nooruddin
5. God's War On Terror by Walid Shoebat/Joel Ricardson
6. Why I Left Jihad by Walid Shoebat
7. For God Or For Tyranny by Walid Shoebat/Theodore Shoebat

The Mormon Books

1. The Book of Doctrine and Covenants
2. The Book of Mormon (another testament of Jesus Christ)
3. By His Own Hand Upon Papyrus by Charles M. Larson
4. Pearl of Great Price
5. Mormon Doctrine by Bruce R. McConkie

The Jehovah Witnesses - Books

1. Millions Now Living Will Never Die
2. New World Translation (NWT)
3. By His Own Hand Upon Papyrus by Charles M. Larson

4. The Kingdom Interlinear Translation of Greek Scriptures
5. Paradise Restored To Mankind by Theocracy!
6. Reasoning From The Scriptures
7. New Heavens and New Earth
8. United in Worship of The Only True God
9. The Truth that Leads to Eternal Life

Unity School Of Christianity - Books

1. Prosperity by Charles Fillmore

Word of Faith - Books

1. Images of Righteousness by Creflo Dollar
2. Authority in Three Worlds by Charles Capps

False Teaching in General - Books

1. The DaVinci CodeBreaker by James L. Garlow

New Age - Books

1. Oprah Miracles And The New Earth by Erwin W. Lutzer

FreeMasons - Books

1. A New Encyclopedia of FreeMasonry by Arthur Edward Waite
2. Revised Duncan's Ritual of Freemasonry pt.1 by Malcom C. Duncan

Jewish - Books

1. Jewish Holy Scriptures by the Army of the United States

Suggested Bibles For Research

Bibles used (includes hardcopy and software copy):
The King James Version (KJV);
The New King James Version; (NKJV)

The English Standard Version (ESV);
The New American Standard Bible (NASB);
The International Version (NIV);
The Revised Standard Version (RSV);
And any others or as many others as you so choose.

Suggested Websites For Research

[*Warning I do not recommend these for new Christians without the guidance of a Sound Biblical Instructor*]

Jehovah Witness material online:

https://www.jw.org/en/
https://www.jw.org/en/publications/bible/
http://www.jwlies.com/

Mormon material online:

https://www.lds.org/?lang=eng
https://www.lds.org/scriptures/pgp?lang=eng
https://www.lds.org/scriptures/bofm?lang=eng
https://www.lds.org/scriptures/dc-testament?lang=eng

Islam material online:

http://www.usc.edu/org/cmje/religious-texts/quran/
https://quran.com/
http://quran.ksu.edu.sa/index.php?l=en#aya=1_1&m=hafs&qaree=husary&trans=en_sh
http://islam.uga.edu/hadith.html
https://sunnah.com/

Masons material online:

http://www.freemasons-freemasonry.com

Resources

Resources

ABOUT THE AUTHORS

About Pastor Robert Anderson

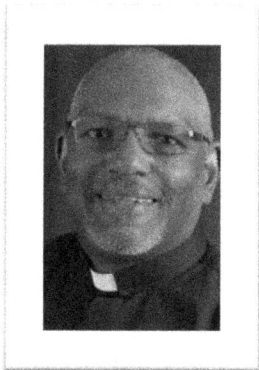

Pastor Robert Anderson is a native of Detroit, Michigan, and has been married to his lovely wife Jo Ann for over 32 years.

Pastor Anderson received his GED, a degree from Wayne County Community College (WC3) in Associate of Applied Science Computer and Data Processing, a degree from Detroit College of Business in Bachelor of Business Administration; and with honors in both degrees.

A salaried employee of AT&T, he learned about diversity through the opportunity to work with people from various cultures and ethnic groups. As he traveled the USA for AT&T, he learned there was more to the world than the streets of Detroit. After several promotions and 30 years of service, Robert chose to retire and pursue his goals as an entrepreneur, professional photographer and videographer.

Pastor Anderson dedicates his life to studying the sound doctrine of Scripture and apologetics with hope of warning and teaching others how to come out of and/or avoid the cults and false doctrine. His first book titled "***Selling Something Nobody Needs, False Doctrine Cleaned Me Up! But God Saved Me!*** is available in bookstores and Amazon.com and the publisher's website www.truthseekersread.com

Today, as a Bible believing Christian he serves as an Associate Pastor licensed under Pastor Emery Moss Jr. at Strictly Biblical Bible Teaching Ministries. Over the years as he has attended various classes and recorded them for his own studies, Pastor Anderson was guided by the Holy Spirit to design a website www.bibletalkbbc.com where various class lectures (audios) and resource literature are available to those that have the desire to learn. And now he has collaborated as co-author and editor of this book with his Pastor and teacher, Pastor Emery Moss Jr.

He and his wife, Jo Ann, witness together at Wendy's, McDonald's and anywhere else they can speak one-on-one and pass out tracts and cards pointing people to Jesus Christ.

You are invited to join Pastor Anderson for his weekly Tele-Conference Bible Study on Tuesdays from 7:00 p.m. – 9:00 p.m. Call in Number (248) 607-0611 /Pin: 14251

For more information or to book Pastor Robert Anderson for speaking engagements, or radio and television interviews, please contact:

Truth Seekers Read, LLC.
P.O. Box 23345, Detroit, MI 48223
Email requests to: truthseekersread@att.net
URL: http://www.truthseekersread.com
Phone: (313) 215-2576

Other Books by Pastor Robert Anderson

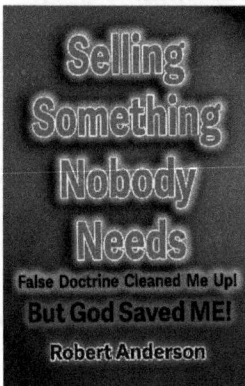

Selling Something
Nobody Needs

False Doctrine Cleaned Me Up!
But God Saved ME!
Robert Anderson

Selling Something Nobody Needs

ISBN: 978-0-9987221-0-8

About Pastor Emery Moss Jr. TH.B., MA

Pastor Emery Moss, Jr. has served as a pastor for over 40 years. Pastor Moss was licensed and ordained as a Full Gospel Non-Denominational Pastor. He went on to serve as Senior Pastor of Christian Fellowship Church in Detroit and Roseville, Michigan for 4 years. From there God called him to do a work at Evangel Ministries in 1985, where he served as an Associate Pastor under the leadership of Pastor Bogel for 11 years. In 1997, Pastor and Sister Moss founded **Strictly Biblical Bible Teaching Ministries,** of Detroit, Michigan, where he now serves as Senior Pastor; located at 10709 Grand River, Detroit, MI 48204. He is also the Founder of Bible Boot Camp Ministries, Inc., where he and his wife, Mary Moss, conduct various seminars on marriage and relationships, as well as cult seminars, etc.   He currently serves as Chaplain of the Dearborn Police Department and Instructor of Human Relations classes for the Dearborn Police Department.

Pastor Moss attended Wayne State University, where he majored in Psychology and Sociology. He graduated from William Tyndale College in Farmington Hills, MI with a Bachelor's Degree in Theology. He also earned a Master's Degree in Biblical Studies from Ashland Theological Seminary in 1998. Pastor Moss has recently received his Diploma in Biblical Counseling from A.A.C.U.

Pastor and Sister Moss have been married for over 40 years.

Pastor Moss has authored several books: "Twisted Teaching of the Word Faith Movement," "Twisted Teaching of the Homosexual Church," and "The Twisted Teaching of the Secret," among others that could be named. Pastor Moss can currently be heard on WLQV radio 1500 AM, Monday—Friday, from 6pm—7pm on the "Bible Talk Show"

For more information or to book Pastor Emery Moss Jr. for speaking engagements, or radio and television interviews, please contact:

Bible Boot Camp Ministries
P.O. Box 05879, Detroit, MI 48205
Email Requests to: bibletalk@bibletalkbbc.com
URL: http://www.bibletalkbbc.com
Phone: (313) 933-9270

BOOK ORDER FORM

Essentials Simple But Biblical

Name: _____

Address: _____

City: _____State: _____Zip: _____

Email: _____

Quantity	
Price (each)	$19.99
Subtotal	
(S&H)	$2.99
MI Tax 6%	
Total	

METHOD OF PAYMENT:

1. **Online Ordering:**
   http://www.truthseekersread.com
2. **Check or Money Order:** (Make payable to: **Truth Seekers Read**)

Mail your Payment with this form to:
Truth Seekers Read, LLC.
P.O. Box 23345, Detroit, MI 48223

Email: truthseekersread@att.net
URL: http://www.truthseekersread.com
Phone: (313) 215-2576

* 9 7 8 0 9 9 8 7 2 2 1 2 2 *